CU01563604

SCOTT KYLE is an award-winning
for his captivating performances
Born and raised in Rutherglen, Sc
a humble beginning to international recognition is an inspir-
ing testament to the power of perseverance and hard work.
He is best known for his roles in *Outlander, The Angels'
Share, Kajaki* and *Singin' I'm No a Billy He's a Tim*. With a
dedicated following of over half a million on social media,
Kyle continues to inspire and entertain audiences worldwide.

For animated summaries of the chapters narrated by the
author, use the QR code below.

It's Not Where You Start

Luath Press Limited

EDINBURGH

www.luath.co.uk

First published 2025

ISBN: 978-1-80425-209-3

This book is made of materials from well-managed, FSC®-certified forests and other controlled sources.

Printed by Ashford Colour Ltd., Gosport

Typeset in 12.5 point Sabon by Lapiz

To everyone I've met along the way – knowingly or not,
you've helped shape this story. Thank you.

Contents

I

It's not show friends, it's show business

It should have been one of the best nights of my life. Another sellout performance of *Singing I'm No a Billy He's a Tim* and, for the first time, all my family was expected to be there to see it.

I had just come off stage from playing to a packed house of more than 3,000 people at the Scottish Exhibition Centre in Glasgow. One of the top venues in the country, the SEC has been played by everyone, including the likes of UB40, Simply Red, The Rolling Stones, Tina Turner, David Bowie and Rod Stewart.

The adrenaline was still coursing through my veins, the laughter and applause were echoing in my ears. I had just taken three curtain calls, with a standing ovation and cheers of 'More! More! Encore!' I was on one of the biggest highs of my life.

Upstairs, in a private room, my long-term girlfriend and future wife Karen and her parents were waiting with my mother, brother and my father's new family – including three sisters and a younger brother I'd never met. They had all been invited by me to watch the show. It was the family reunion I had been praying for since I was a kid and they were all there to celebrate with me. I knew it was going to be a night to remember, and I was right.

Just before heading to the party I took time to have a chat with Des Dillon, the author of the play I had just performed and the man I looked upon as a friend, mentor and almost surrogate father-figure.

I often used to call Des at the end of a performance to tell him how well the show had gone but this night was different. It was one of the biggest audiences we had ever played to and Des had been in the audience, which made it even more special.

As we were packing up the set and loading it into the van Des came up on stage and said he had something to tell me. The adrenaline was still pumping through my veins and I was eager to get his reaction to the performance, which had gone exceptionally well. I thought Des would be pleased and I was right. In fact he was so pleased he told me he was pulling the plug and taking the show away from me.

Suddenly, instead of being upstairs with my family and celebrating a pinnacle of my success, I was alone in the lobby of a theatre trying to get my head around the realisation that my world had just collapsed. Everything I had worked for over the previous five years, along with all my dreams and ambitions for the show, were vanishing in the blink of an eye.

'It's nothing personal,' said Des. 'I've just decided that I want to take back production of the show and put it on myself.'

After five years he was exercising his right to take back his play. He was perfectly entitled to do this, after all we didn't have a long-term written agreement.

My head was spinning. I understood exactly what he was saying but, in my mind, I was like a passenger on the stricken *Titanic* searching frantically for a lifebelt; I was desperately trying to find a way out that would prevent me from drowning.

I could hear Des talking, I could see his lips moving, but the words weren't making much sense. He was calmly explaining why he wanted to take back control of the show but my thoughts, and my heart, were racing. Sweat was starting to form on my brow and my blood was boiling. Visions of the last five years were flowing through my mind, like a dying man watching life pass before his eyes.

Flashes of memories assailed my brain. I remembered the day I discovered the play during a visit to the library and my excitement upon realising it was something I could relate to, and of rushing home to rehearse it with friends in my tiny 10ft by 9ft bedroom.

I thought of the nights I had spent stacking shelves in a supermarket to raise the money for marketing materials, of trudging round pubs begging them to let me put on the show in run-down back rooms to a handful of people. The hours I spent building up interest with major theatres, of walking mile after mile in the rain, sun and howling gales to push flyers through letterboxes in towns all over Scotland just to get ordinary folk to come and see the show.

It was more than a play to me, it was what made me get up in the morning. It had helped me win 'The Stage Award for Acting Excellence – Best Actor' award for my performance at the Edinburgh Fringe Festival. I hadn't just put time, money, blood, sweat and tears into producing it. I had invested my soul.

I had taken that play from nothing to playing in front of 3,000 people and grossing £50,000 a night. It had earned over £1 million at the box office and become one of Scottish theatre's greatest success stories of recent times. And it had all been done without any funding or outside financial support.

Now, in a conversation lasting less than three minutes, everything I had worked almost a fifth of my life for was finished.

What was I going to tell Karen? What was I going to tell the rest of my family? They were all waiting upstairs in the private bar celebrating a success which, at this precise instant, now felt more like failure. I'm not sure I have ever felt as rejected and devastated as I did at that moment. Now I understood completely the saying: 'It's not show friends, it's show business'.

The walk from the stage, out along the concourse of the SEC, to where my family and friends were waiting was only a couple of hundred yards but it was one of the longest and loneliest I've ever made.

Climbing the stairs to the first floor I felt like a condemned man mounting the scaffold. It wasn't just myself I felt sorry for. I knew my family and the friends who had helped me get this far would also be devastated.

People like me weren't supposed to be successful. I was an ordinary guy from a broken home in a working-class area of Glasgow. It was alright to have dreams and ambitions, like millions of other people, but nobody really expected them to come true. In achieving what I had, however minor that was, I had broken a mould and become an exception to the rule.

I knew I had been lucky and that whatever success I had enjoyed was shared by my family and friends. I had gone from working in a shop on minimum wage to earning enough money to be able to pay off my mum's mortgage and settle all her debts. I was on the verge of setting up home with Karen and starting a new life, perhaps even a family.

My dad used to play in bands with dreams of making it big that were never realised. My mum wrote poetry but was too shy to share it or get published. Here I was, standing on a stage getting applause from thousands of people, and I knew they were proud of me. In a small way I hoped they could experience a little of their own dreams through me. How was I going to tell them it was all over?

As I approached the door to the room I could hear the sound of chatter and laughter but my heart was heavy. I couldn't say anything now, I had to keep the news to myself for a little longer and not spoil the party.

As my hand reached for the door handle I took a deep breath, said to myself, 'It's show time!' and walked into the room with the biggest smile possible and my arms open wide, like I was making a grand stage entrance.

For the rest of the evening I laughed and joked with everyone as if nothing was wrong. All the time there was a sickening feeling in the pit of my stomach and a lump in my throat. I may have been surrounded by people but I felt very much alone.

Now I realise it was possibly the best performance I've ever given and one that changed my life. Somewhere, from deep within my subconscious, the lyrics of 'It's Not Where You Start', a song from the old Broadway musical, *Seesaw*, kept getting louder and louder in my head.

That's when I knew I wasn't finished yet.

2

Glasgow's Miles Better

Glasgow in the 1970s and early 1980s was a much different city to the one it is today. The former workshop of the world and second city of the British empire, which had produced some of the greatest ships in history and whose name was a byword for manufacturing quality, was going through a major readjustment.

The economics and politics of the day had closed the gates on many of the old ways. Men who had worked all their lives in the shipyards of the Clyde or in other industrial manufacturing workplaces, just as their fathers and grand-fathers had done before them, were suddenly out of a job.

It was a dark period in the history of the city. Mass unem-ployment coupled with high levels of urban decay was eating away at communities where, in some places, youngsters with nothing better to do formed gangs and indulged in petty but violent tribal warfare.

Stabbings were commonplace, often fuelled by excessive alcohol consumption, as Glasgow earned the dubious title of being the knife crime capital of Europe.

The 1970s were especially bad. It was a decade of decay. Areas of Glasgow were immersed in a level of deprivation that is hard to imagine today.

It seems incredible now, when you think what the city is like today, but back then there was still a lot of poverty and damp, run-down, vermin-infested slum housing. Entire fam-ilies lived in one or two rooms without the basic necessities of running water and electricity.

Although efforts were being made to transform the city, progress was slow. Huge areas of slum housing were sys-tematically being demolished and the occupants moved into high-rise apartments, or relocated to massive new pur-pose-built housing estates – or 'schemes' as they are called in Glasgow – outside the city centre. The intention to give people somewhere decent to live was honourable but these schemes ended up promising much more than they would eventually deliver. In the race to build homes the designers seemed to forget that communities also need shops, pubs and other facilities if they are to thrive.

While all this was going on there was still a lot of rising unemployment and industrial discontent which led to endless disputes and strikes. In 1975 Glasgow's bin men downed tools for 13 weeks, resulting in the city's streets being swamped with rotting garbage.

Rats and flies thrived as children were forced to play in filthy, foul-smelling backyards amid piles of rubbish. It was estimated that every day the strike went on more than 1,000 tons of waste was being dumped in the streets and threatening an epidemic of disease. For the first time in 25 years the army had to be called in to deal with an industrial dispute and help clear up a mountain of more than 70,000 tons of rotting rubbish.

It was a pattern of despair that would continue for the rest of the decade. Continuous strikes among public sector workers over low pay and poor conditions, rocketing inflation and rising unemployment took its toll on the city.

By the end of the 1970s it seemed everyone was suffering as the morale of the country reached its lowest point for more than 200 years.

It was during this period of chaos and uncertainty that my parents went through their most formative teenage years.

My mother and father were both children of the Sixties. Mum was born Joyce Wilson in 1961 in Rottenrow Hospital, Glasgow, two years after my dad, James, came into the world 12 miles away at Ross Hospital in Paisley. Both institutions are now long gone.

Children of their generation from areas like ours were not expected to go to university and even though many were certainly bright enough very few families had the financial means to afford it. They were at best factory fodder, but there weren't any factories anymore.

They met when my mum, the youngest of seven children, was just 16 years old and my dad, the oldest of three, was only 17.

It wasn't exactly a whirlwind romance but within six months they were married. It was a union of hope over experience as neither had any real idea of what they were signing up for.

In many ways I think their marriage was an escape from reality and an attempt to live a fantasy of sorts – the only trouble was they didn't necessarily share the same vision.

From what I have learned since, from speaking to both of them individually, it was a relationship doomed from the start. They obviously cared for each other and probably thought it was love but, with the benefit of hindsight, it's now clear their experiences growing up had created different expectations. For the next few years they endured a volatile relationship as they tried to make a life together in a city weighed down by an image of negativity, violence and despair.

Glasgow wasn't a positive place back then. For many people the dream was to get out of it. It certainly wasn't as attractive a city as it is today and it didn't draw the attention of many visitors. A weekend break was something more usually associated with a hospital-treated fracture, following a Friday night on the drink, rather than a holiday.

However, there were some people who realised the city needed a new image if it was going to have a brighter future.

Inspiration for change came from New York. The most populous city in America had also been going through a tough time in the Seventies. The economy was on the verge of bankruptcy, crime was rampant and tourism was at an all-time low. In many ways just like Glasgow.

In an attempt to reverse the negative reputation a campaign was launched to encourage more people to visit the Big Apple. It was graphic designer Milton Glaser who came up with the idea of the logo and slogan 'I Love New York' and it was an instant hit.

Glasgow needed to do something similar that would be equally simple, relatable, eye-catching and, most importantly, positive, if it was to shrug off its stereotypical image of being a redundant, run-down, violent city.

Glasgow was desperately trying to clean up its buildings and its act in an attempt to portray itself as a vibrant city of culture and enterprise. Any major marketing campaign needed to promote the merits and attractions of the 'dear green place', as the city has historically been called, and to demonstrate to the world the changes taking place.

The resulting 'Glasgow's Miles Better' campaign, promoted by the then Lord Provost Dr Michael Kelly and PR man Harry Diamond, caught the imagination of the world.

Within days of its launch more than 25,000 bumper stickers were handed out to Glaswegians and the slogan was translated into French, Italian and other languages. Sightings of the logo were recorded as far away as the Himalayas and Russia.

The campaign, which has since gone down in history as one of the best promotions ever mounted by a city, led to Glasgow hosting a major National Garden Festival on the old docklands in 1987. That was followed by Glasgow being named European City of Culture and European City of Architecture in the 1990s and European Capital of Sport in 2003.

Over the last 40 years Glasgow has changed enormously. Where once there were derelict shipyards and abandoned docks, there is now a thriving hub of creativity, entertainment venues and luxury residential properties.

The city is globally recognised as a leading centre for contemporary music. It has produced internationally acclaimed artists and is home to the SSE Hydro – the third busiest music venue in the world.

Much of this amazing transformation can be traced back to a single day in history.

Monday 27 June 1983 was a big day for Glasgow. It was the date the Provost Dr Michael Kelly officially declared 'Glasgow's miles better' as he helped hoist a giant smiley face cartoon character onto the front of the City Chambers to announce the rebirth of Glasgow.

Serendipitously, it was also the day I came into the world.

3
We are all the sum of our parts

As I've grown older, and hopefully wiser, I've come to realise we are all the sum of our parts.

To understand what makes us who we are it is often useful to learn a little of what happened before we were born. The life experiences of our parents can have a very profound impact on our own personalities, attitudes and behaviour.

Even though for more than 20 years I hardly saw him, my father has cast a giant shadow over my life.

He and my mother split up when I was little more than a baby. As a child I would sit for hours at the window waiting in vain for him to visit. I would go through ridiculous superstitious rituals; maybe if I sat with my legs crossed in a certain way he would come because that's how I was sitting the last time he visited.

At school I would make up fanciful stories about him being a rich businessman with a private jet who was always working abroad on some major deal. I could never understand what I had done that was so wrong that he didn't want to see me.

Only now, as I have got to know him through adult eyes and discovered what made him the man he is, can I finally understand what went wrong and why he walked away from my brother and me. I have learned to forgive even though I'll never forget.

It was only recently that I discovered just how difficult my father's life had been and the circumstances that made him stay away for so long. Sitting in a pub, sipping an orange juice, my father told me things he had never spoken about to my mother, knowledge he had kept bottled up for decades but that had shaped his views and some of his actions.

My dad was born James Kyle in the Ross Hospital, Paisley on 17 July 1959. His mother, Mary, worked in a dry-cleaning shop while his dad, James, was a postman.

By all accounts his parents appear to have had something of a turbulent relationship, built on lies and deception.

When he was about seven or eight years old my dad over-heard his mother confiding in a friend a secret that rocked his world and impacted his self-worth for years afterwards.

Late one night, while he was in bed supposedly sleeping, his parents were entertaining friends when he heard his mother's voice coming from the hallway. He could just about make out her whispering to one of her pals. It was obviously an interesting conversation and their hushed tones made him even more curious.

What he heard was a bombshell. Without having to strain much to catch the conversation he listened to his mum admit to her friend that the man he thought was his father wasn't.

To learn the man he called dad wasn't his biological father was absolutely devastating.

What made it worse was that he wasn't supposed to know. It was a secret he had to live with and could never talk about to anybody. He never even told my mother.

I was shocked when he told me, and upset for him that he had felt forced to keep something like that to himself for so many years. However, it did go a long way to clarifying some of the events in my childhood.

It also helped explain why my grandparents' relationship had been so rocky. By the time my father had reached the age of 12 my grandmother Mary had met another man and my grandfather had walked out on his children.

Unfortunately, rather than making life more peaceful, the break-up of the family, however dysfunctional it had been, turned out to be the start of another nightmare for my dad.

Drink was a big part of the culture in Glasgow when he was growing up and both his mother and her new man were very heavy drinkers. There were numerous occasions when my dad and his two younger sisters, Andrea, aged ten, and eight-year-old Wilma, were left to go hungry because all the money that came into the house had been spent on alcohol.

Things eventually got so bad that while my dad was still only 12 years old, he was forced to take on the role as the main carer for his sisters.

My grandmother was clearly an alcoholic. She got involved with a clique of around ten other very heavy drinkers who would pool their cash for booze. Each day one of the gang would go and claim their money for unemployment, or whatever benefits they were on, and then buy drink for the group. They would then spend their days at each other's homes drinking themselves into oblivion.

Often, when there was no food in the house, my dad would have to sit and wait until his mother passed out from the drink before raiding her handbag to steal enough money to buy food for his sisters and himself.

The responsibility of looking after his siblings meant he rarely attended school. To all intents and purposes he quit full-time education at the age of 12, at a time when the legal minimum age to leave school was 16.

In order to feed his sisters and keep a roof over their heads he lied about his age to get a job. He walked miles and miles for days on end across Glasgow, knocking on doors, calling into shops and stopping by industrial sheds begging anyone to give him a chance. After weeks of trying, he finally found an opening with a bakery delivering bread.

For almost three years he worked long hours with the bakery and undertook a number of other unskilled jobs just to support himself and his sisters while his mother continued to drink her life away.

Finally, when he was 15, he had had enough. He had always known there was something far wrong with the whole situation but he had been too busy trying to survive and protect his sisters to realise the toll it was taking on his own wellbeing.

It was then that he faced up to the reality that his mother, aunt and grandmother were all functioning alcoholics.

During the week they were all nice, friendly, happy people but the minute they got a drink in them at the weekend it would all kick off. They spent the time getting drunk and fighting with their men or amongst themselves. It was constant conflict. Almost every weekend the police would be called to intervene in some violent argument, sometimes so out of hand that somebody would end up getting stabbed.

By and large when it comes to alcohol there are two kinds of people, happy drunks and violent drunks. Unfortunately his family all belonged to the second set.

It was the culture of the time in the society he was growing up in. There was nothing else for people to do. When my dad finally realised the people who were supposed to love and look after him were obsessed with drinking and preferred getting drunk and fighting to living a 'normal' life, he left his mother's home to go and stay with his Aunt Betty in Castlemilk. She was only six years older than my dad and was often out at work or partying with her friends, so to all intents and purposes he was on his own.

He rarely saw my grandmother again, only taking my brother Craig and myself to see her a couple of times. I never enjoyed those visits. The house was always smoky, the walls covered in yellow nicotine stains and it smelled of drink.

The last time they met was when she was in hospital. They hadn't spoken for three years when he got the call that she was nearing the end of life. Against his better judgement he felt obligated to visit.

When he went to the hospital she was sleeping so he took a chair and sat by her side for several hours. When she woke up and saw him by the bed there was no Hollywood reconciliation or final expressions of love. Her only words were, 'Fuck, if you're here I must be dying!'

Those were the last words she ever said to him. She passed about two hours later. Even after all she put him through

I know he was really hurt by it and still has regrets that he didn't try harder to help her.

I doubt there was much he could have done. She was an alcoholic who didn't want to be helped. When he broke free at the age of 15, he did it for his own survival. To make such a decision at any time is never easy but it must have been especially hard for him as a young teenager in the Glasgow of 1974.

Despite the scarcity of employment my dad scoured the city for work. It was very difficult getting a job in Glasgow at that time. There had been a lot of strikes, the coal miners, postmen and others, as well as numerous factory closures and lay-offs. A lot of guys had been out of work for months so there was a lot of competition for a limited number of jobs.

However, one thing he and I share is a determination to do what it takes to realise our goals. Once again, he walked miles, knocking on doors, going unannounced into shops and yards to ask for a job. Eventually he found himself in an office in Pollok-shaws. The owner didn't have any vacancies but was impressed by my dad's attitude. He called up a friend who owned a glazing firm in Kinning Park and put a word in for him. Suddenly, after weeks of trudging the streets, more in hope than anticipation, my dad had managed to secure a four-year apprenticeship as a glazier. For the first time in his life things were looking positive. He had escaped his chaotic, violent family life and got a good job with prospects. He was, he felt, on the up!

However, there was still something missing. Looking back he admits now that he didn't know exactly what he wanted. All he knew was that there had to be a better way of living, one that he had never experienced before. He found it with my mum's family.

4
Sadie The Lady

My mother's upbringing could not have been more different to my dad's. While he was born into a chaotic, often violent and unstable domestic environment fuelled by alcohol abuse, my mother, Joyce, came from a much more secure and happy family background.

The lynchpin of the household, and the glue that held the smooth running of the Wilson family together, was my grandmother, Sarah, who I used to call Sadie the Lady.

The product of Irish immigrants to Glasgow in the early 1900s, Sadie's early life had been hard but happy, despite the undoubted poverty she was born into.

She arrived in this world as Sarah Veronica Gilmour Nicoll on 7 August 1923, the second of four surviving children. Two older siblings died in infancy before Sadie was born, an all-too-common occurrence at the time. There was hardly a family in Glasgow, or anywhere in Scotland, that didn't share similar stories. There just wasn't the medical knowledge or access to treatment that we have today.

Sadie was lucky to survive. When she was very young she suffered from a bout of Diphtheria, a highly infectious and dangerous disease which was rife in Glasgow in the 1920s. It accounted for a large proportion of the city's high childhood mortality rate as it usually claimed the lives of more than 40 per cent of those who got infected. Her most abiding memory of the time was having to spend days in a steam tent in hospital after having her tonsils and adenoids removed as part of the treatment for the disease.

It wasn't just the children who were at risk of premature death. The average life expectancy of a working-class man in Glasgow at the time was about 48 years. Her father didn't even make that.

The sudden death of her beloved dad, Henry, at the age of just 42 was one of the biggest blows of her early life and it hit her very hard. He had worked in a galvanising works where fumes from the industrial process were suspected of giving him heart problems, or at least making any undiagnosed existing condition worse.

The day he died, on Sunday 4 December 1932, Sadie was just nine years old. She had been getting ready to go to a church parade and was dressed in her Brownies uniform when there was a knock on the door. It was a policeman who had called to tell her mother, Janet, that Henry had collapsed at work and had died in hospital earlier that day.

Even though it was a tremendous shock, Sadie said her mother insisted she, and her brother and sisters, should carry on and attend the church service. She remembered there was a Christening, which made her sad because part of the sermon given by the priest talked about 'one life ending as another begins'.

On the way back from the church her little three-year-old sister, May, started singing a traditional lullaby, 'Baby's Eyes Are Irish', which her Ballymena-born father had taught her. It was a highly emotional moment as the song contains the line: '*Daddy's gone to heaven, he's gone to paradise, leaving his poor little baby, with lovely blue Irish eyes.*' Sadie said everyone started to cry, including the Sunday school teachers.

The loss of her father meant Sadie's mum was left on her own, bringing up four children in a first-floor flat in one of the old brown stone tenement buildings where they shared a toilet with eight other families. Their home had just two bedrooms, a living room and a kitchen with a bed in it. That's where her mother slept while Sadie and her brother and sisters had the bedrooms.

They never had much money but they were a close-knit family and it instilled in my grandmother the importance of love and stability. Sadie stayed there until she was 19. She only moved out when she married my grandfather, Charlie Wilson, and they set up their own home.

Sadie was only 16 when she met 22-year-old Charlie at a dance in 1939. Glasgow was renowned for its dance halls and movie theatres back then and Sadie always loved to dance.

Their wartime romance was made easier as my grandfather Charlie was unfit for military service. He was stone deaf, a lifelong condition resulting from an early childhood ear infection that was never properly treated. It didn't help that for a long time he wore his hearing aid in the wrong ear. When he did eventually change it, he managed to get a little bit more hearing, but not much. He could not hear you if your back was turned. Incredibly, even though he could not hear the music to dance to, he and my grandmother were brilliant together. She would tap him on the shoulder and he would feel the vibration of the music through the floor. By all accounts, friends and family who saw them together said they moved beautifully around the dance floor, but my grandfather never heard a note.

When it came to everyday conversation he had developed his own form of sign language which he used to communicate with friends and family.

He had also lost part of a finger in an industrial accident some years before the war. Anyway, as an experienced metal turner and lathe operator he was far more valuable on the home front.

They courted for a couple of years and married on Friday 7 August 1942 shortly after Sadie turned 19. It was a happy union and they stayed together for over 45 years until Charlie died in 1987 aged 69.

Like many couples at the time their life together started rather humbly. Being a wartime marriage the ceremony was pretty basic, a far cry from the sun-kissed beach on Cyprus where Karen and I tied the knot some 71 years later.

Sadie and Charlie's wedding celebration was a simple affair. A brief service followed by a meal with a handful of guests in a Glasgow city centre tearoom, and then a night at the theatre to see Sadie's favourite singer of the day, the Scottish tenor Monte Rey. The weekend was rounded off with a brief honeymoon in Edinburgh before getting back to work and the war effort on the Monday morning.

For a newlywed couple in Glasgow of 1942 Sadie and Charlie were incredibly lucky to find somewhere to live. Only a year earlier, in March 1941, two nights of German bombing, known as the Clydebank Blitz, had killed over 1,200 people and left a further 35,000 homeless. That was only one of 11 air raids on the city during the war which inflicted massive casualties and destroyed thousands of residential buildings.

At the time Sadie and Charlie were looking for a home they were up against 28 other applicants desperately vying for the one room and a kitchen, with a toilet, that they eventually got. Situated in the less than salubrious area of Gallowgate, about a mile from the city centre, their families were not keen on them taking it but there was no alternative.

Despite the limited space it was to be home for the next 16 years as they started a family of their own. By the time they moved to a bigger place in 1956 Sadie and Charlie had been living in the one room with up to four children.

Mind you, family life didn't start easily for them. Two years after they were married Sadie fell pregnant with their first child, Derek. Sadly, he was born prematurely on 12 March 1944 and only lived for ten minutes.

One of the most heartbreaking stories she ever told me was about that day. Sadie had to be rushed into hospital as she had developed problems with the pregnancy and gone into labour early. My grandfather was contacted at work and rushed to be by her side.

Soon after he arrived Derek died and even though he had just lost his son he was expected to go back to work that afternoon. He wasn't allowed to spend any time comforting his devastated wife.

For Sadie it was even worse. She was immediately put on a ward with other mums and their newborns. Within hours of losing her own child a nurse came along and gave her somebody else's baby to feed because she had milk. She wasn't given time to grieve properly. As hard as it is to comprehend now it's just how things were done in those days.

Fortunately Sadie and Charlie went on to have more children, two boys and four girls over the next 15 years, culminating with my mother Joyce, the baby of the family.

By the time my mum arrived on the scene the Wilson family had moved from Gallowgate in the city centre to the more open spaces of Castlemilk, which at the time was one of the biggest housing schemes in Europe.

They had swapped their one room and a kitchen for a three-bedroomed flat. Sadie was in seventh heaven; it was the first home she had lived in with an indoor bathroom since getting married.

Overall, the Wilson family rubbed along pretty well together at the Tormusk Road address for the next 21 years.

My mum was born on 23 March 1961 – a full 15 years and one day after her oldest surviving sibling, Janette, was born on 24 March 1946.

Between the mid-1940s and early '50s my grandparents had a child almost every two years. Grace was born in 1948, Charles, or Chick as he was known, arrived in 1950, Norma in 1952 and then John in 1958.

By the time my mother reached her teenage years in the 1970s all but John were married and had left home. Instead of brothers and sisters my mum often felt as though she had several sets of parents telling her what to do and trying to give advice. It was a situation she didn't enjoy and wasn't always willing to accept.

My mum, who became very close to her parents in later life, admits that as a teenager she was pretty wilful and embarrassed at having an older mother. She resented the fact all of her friends had younger, trendier parents and felt ashamed if her mother came to school looking more like her pals' granny than a mum.

In many ways my mother missed the drama that she saw happening in other families around her. She didn't like the boring, staid, comfortable, organised and predictable life at home. She craved some kind of excitement.

It was that teenage angst, coupled with a lack of self-confidence, that caused her to seek an escape from the kind of life that my father so desperately longed to find for himself. It was never going to end well.

5

Teenage romances seem to be a thing in my family

When Jimmy met Joyce it was hardly the stuff of romantic comedy, more the opening scenes of a disaster movie when you just know that something is going to go wrong.

They were just 16 and 17 years old. Dad was a street-smart lad about town with a job, money and was driving around in a car, even though he didn't have a licence. He was playing in a rock band and leading an independent life. Mum was a bored, frustrated teenager, working as an assistant in a shoe shop but embarrassed about living at home with an older mother and father the same age as her friends' grandparents.

Listening to each of them talk about how they met it's clear there weren't any lightning bolts of love at first sight, or even any true love at all. It was more a shared feeling of mutual envy. Each saw something in the life of the other they desperately wanted for themselves.

They first set eyes on one another while hanging out on a street corner, as is often the case for youngsters who feel they are too old for youth clubs but too young to legally go into pubs. My mother had been standing talking to friends when my dad walked past with one of his mates and they got chatting.

Neither had been in a relationship before and it was exciting. As the weeks progressed their friendship developed. My mum and her pals would go and visit my dad when his aunt was out. It was somewhere to socialise free from the glare of watchful parents, a convenient place where they could chat freely, play music and enjoy an illicit drink.

Conversely, my mum would invite my dad home and he would get a chance to sit down at a dinner table and join in the kind of family activities he had never experienced before, like sitting as a group to watch television and just talking about everyday things without it all flaring up into an argument.

After just a few weeks of going steady my mum decided she wanted a wedding and they announced plans to get married. My grandparents tried very hard to talk them out of it and even encouraged a long engagement but my mum was having none of it. It caused a terrible row which only served to make my mother even more determined.

For his part, my dad was happy to go along with it. Whenever he stayed over, sharing a room with my mum's brother as anything else would have been improper, he was treated to cooked meals and my grandmother Sadie would make him packed lunches to take to work. She would even do some of his laundry.

Added to that, my grandfather Charlie would take him to play snooker once a week in the local club. It was a bonding experience he had never had with his own family. It was what he had been longing for.

On 11 November 1976, less than six months after they first met, my 16-year-old mum and 17-year-old dad were married at Martha Street Registrar office. They were almost the same ages my wife Karen and I were when we met, but in reverse. I was 16 to her 18. Teenage romances seem to be a thing in my family!

Life was very good for the newlyweds at first, even though they had to move in with my grandparents because it was almost impossible to get a council flat at that time, especially at such a young age.

They both admit now, with the benefit of hindsight, that the marriage was a mistake but my mum had got what she desired, a chance to rebel against her parents and experience the dream of living a grown-up life. And my dad was happy because he had been welcomed into the family and treated like a son.

The trouble was that although they both got what they needed they wanted different things. My mother was after freedom, not a husband, and he didn't want a wife. He was looking for a mother.

The first few months of married life really was a honeymoon period. While they were living with my grandparents everything was good and both have very fond memories of those days. The rot only started to set in once they got a place of their own.

My mother was adamant she wanted to be mistress in her own home and embarked on a mission to find a flat. In 1977 they got lucky. She had spent weeks writing to community councillors, the local member of parliament and as many people she could think of asking for help. Eventually they were offered a couple of rooms in an old tenement block. The flat needed a lot of work but they grabbed the opportunity with both hands and set about trying to make it into a home with bits and pieces of furniture donated by friends and relatives.

Once they started to settle down into everyday life, the tiny cracks in their relationship turned into giant canyons.

Like a lot of young, working-class men of the time with ambitions for a better life my dad saw two potential avenues of escape from poverty. One was to play professional football, the other was to become a rock star. My dad's dreams pointed towards the second option.

Much to the irritation of the neighbours he stepped up his ambition to become a drummer, playing in a succession of local bands. Every weekend he would be out performing in pubs, clubs, at weddings or any kind of gig that would provide a few extra pounds in his pocket and maybe lead to the big time.

But, while he was out living the rock star life my mum would be left at home on her own. What young woman is going to be happy with that while her partner is out at a pub surrounded by lots of happy people having fun? It was a recipe for disaster.

According to my dad the main reasons he didn't take my mum with him was that she was, initially, too young to be

legally allowed in pubs where most of the gigs were played.
When she turned 18 and that excuse was no longer valid he
said it was because she couldn't handle her drink. Coupled
with a short temper alcohol could turn her aggressive and
she might cause a scene. He had seen too much of that as a
young boy and didn't want a repeat performance.

I'm sure there were other reasons too, not least because
it's very easy, when you are young and full of confidence to
start believing your own publicity. There are few young men
who wouldn't like being surrounded by people full of praise
for their performance or being chatted up by girls flirting
with members of the band. It was all too easy to get carried
away and he admits he sometimes let his vanity take over.

Show business became everything to my dad. He was
always trying to go that stage further, to get a unique sound
or different look for the bands he was playing in. When
he was a boy he was constantly told he wouldn't achieve
anything but at last he thought he had found a niche and
wanted to prove his critics wrong. He enjoyed performing
and he was good at it.

My dad's obsession with the 'rock star' lifestyle meant he
was increasingly away from home at weekends, playing one-
night gigs in countless pubs and clubs across the country.
One night he would be in Newcastle and the next in Dundee.
It affected his marriage and his work.

More than a few times he managed to get fired from his
day job because he had turned up late too many times for
work, having been gigging all weekend. He was sacked once
for borrowing the work's van and sloping off early on a Friday afternoon to drive the band and all its equipment hundreds of miles across country to play in a pub somewhere.

Another time he was fired after taking the work's van
to a Sunday night gig in England. By the time he got back
to Glasgow it was almost dawn and he decided to try and

grab a couple of hours sleep. Unfortunately his 8am alarm failed and he didn't wake up until 9.30am. When he looked out the window of his flat the van was gone. He was ecstatic as he thought he now had the perfect excuse for being late for work – somebody had stolen the van. However, when he phoned the office to tell them the news he learned it was his boss who had collected it at 8am that morning and that he was sacked again.

My dad ended up getting the boot from so many glazing companies in Glasgow that it was difficult to find one that would have him. He ended up working for a company selling soft drinks door-to-door before eventually becoming a taxi driver.

His constant absences also took their toll on my mother. She started drinking more, going out with her pals or hosting parties in the flat while my dad was away. Through the week, when neither of them were drinking, they got on great but at weekends they lived almost separate existences.

Inevitably, they started to argue and fight. They would break-up and one of them would move out. But, within a few weeks, they would inevitably get back together. It was a continuous cycle, a destructive pattern doomed to repeat itself again and again over the next few years.

They both cheated on each other during their separations and when the drink flowed those indiscretions would be used as weapons in arguments that would blow up, seemingly out of nowhere.

During one of their many reconciliations my brother Craig was conceived so they got back together. For a time at least they were happy. Mum was pregnant and wasn't drinking while Dad had newfound responsibilities.

When Craig was born in April 1981 they got a new council flat in Castlemilk and managed to stay together for about a year. Eventually the old destructive pattern began again.

My dad was still trying to be a rock star and my mum hankered for the single teenage years she had missed out on.

They were children having children. It got to the point they couldn't have a civilised conversation because too much water had passed under the bridge. They had caused each other too much pain.

I have no doubt my parents cared for each other in their own peculiar ways, they just couldn't live together. However, it didn't stop them trying one last time. Sometime around the end of 1982 during one of their brief reconciliations I was conceived.

Looking back on it all, as objectively as possible, what I find most incredible is that in so many ways it was a miracle I was born at all.

6

My debut on the world stage

As almost every actor knows, a spectacular entrance is often the key to an engaging performance. So, when you consider the circumstances of my debut on the world stage I sometimes wonder if perhaps I was always destined for the theatre. Certainly my first appearance in the spotlight was a little more dramatic than some.

On the evening of 26 June 1983 my nine-months pregnant mum was at home in the two-bedroom flat in Govanhill that she was sharing with my brother Craig and my father – on the rare occasions when he was around during one of their sporadic reunions.

That night my dad was out working as a taxi driver when Mum went into labour. I wasn't due for another few days so when her waters broke it was a bit of a surprise. My grandparents, Sadie and Charlie, had gone away on holiday – starting a trend that continued throughout my life. Sadie always missed my birthday because she was on vacation.

In those days a lot of families didn't have telephones in their home, not everyone could afford such an expensive luxury, especially in Govanhill which has long since been considered one of the most deprived communities in Scotland.

It was also way before personal cell phones had been invented. If anybody had told my mother back then that everybody would soon be carrying a phone in their pocket, and could be contactable 24 hours a day almost anywhere in the world, she would have thought they were on drugs or suffering from delusions.

My brother was only two years old at the time so my mum was effectively on her own when the contractions began. With no-one around to help her she had to carry Craig down two flights of stairs and walk him to the end of the road where there was a public telephone.

Despite being in a lot of discomfort and pain she managed to struggle to the call box and dialled the office of the taxi firm where my dad was working. She was getting increasingly anxious and impatient to get hold of him so he could come home and take her to hospital.

But my dad wasn't there. He was out on a job, collecting the owner of the taxi firm that employed him from a club in Glasgow. The reason the switchboard operator couldn't reach him was that he had gone into the venue to fetch his boss and had been forced to wait for almost an hour.

Desperate for help, as clearly I wasn't prepared to wait to make my big entrance, my mum had to call an ambulance. Within minutes she was speeding through the streets of Glasgow, with blue lights flashing and sirens wailing, to Rutherglen Maternity Hospital.

By the time my dad got the message my mum was already at the maternity unit. He quickly dropped off his fare and raced to the hospital. According to him he must have broken numerous laws getting there as he shot through red lights, took corners on two wheels and shattered the speed limit as he tore through the streets of Glasgow.

When he finally did get to the labour ward the nurse accused him of being late because he had 'probably been out drinking' and tried to get him thrown out of the hospital. Luckily he managed to convince her that he was stone-cold sober and he made it just in time for my first appearance, sometime shortly before 2am on the morning of 27 June 1983.

Obviously I don't really have many memories of family life in Govanhill, I was only there for a couple of years before we moved, but I do have a very vague recollection of being pushed in a baby buggy as my mum walked Craig to primary school, of attending a local play group and playing on the furniture in the front room.

Every Sunday we would go to my gran's home for lunch. I remember playing on the veranda with my grandfather and sitting in the kitchen, watching the windows steam up as the dinner was being cooked and Sadie singing along to Elvis, Jim Reeves and Nat King Cole.

Sadie played a big part in my life then and right up until her death aged 93 in February 2017. My gran always seemed happy and positive. I never heard her say anything bad about anyone and she always had favourite little phrases that made me laugh. If someone was saying something negative about someone or a situation she would say, 'There is nought as queer as folk'. If she thought someone was exaggerating a story she would say, 'Yer bum's oot the winda'. If my brother and I were making too much noise or demanding a lot of her attention she would say, 'Give me peace in my own house'.

She would always try to guide us in the right direction without ever appearing to be giving advice. Maybe she's the reason I'm attracted to older souls. She never made me feel she was judging me about anything if I went to talk to her about problems.

All my memories of this early time in my life are happy ones, maybe because I was too young to understand what was really going on around me.

My parents' relationship had been rocky for years. They had gone through repeated separations and reconciliations which only resulted in them continuing to grow further and further apart. Each time they split up it became more difficult to get back together again and there was an awful lot of pent-up hostility which I didn't comprehend as a child. It's only with hindsight and talking to my parents as an adult that I have been able to piece together my rose-tinted fragments of memories into a picture that is nearer to the truth.

In many ways I'm glad I only remember the good moments as by all accounts things were far from happy at home at this time. My brother, being that little bit older, has more realistic memories, which probably explains why he never had the same longing to reconnect with our father that I had.

According to my dad he was trying to find some stability in his life around the time things really came to a head with my mum. He had developed a very low tolerance for being around drunk people. And, considering his family background, it is easy to understand why he might have taken such a position but it also set him on a collision course with my mother. She had not had the same negative relationship with alcohol growing up and saw nothing wrong in having a drink, even if it didn't always agree with her.

One of final nails in the relationship coffin happened one weekend after my dad had just come back from playing a Saturday night gig in Newcastle to perform at a pub in Glasgow on the Sunday evening. He hadn't seen my mum all weekend and she was clearly upset at having been left on her own so had got in a babysitter and gone out drinking with friends.

By the time she got to the pub where my dad was performing, the drink had fuelled her anger and jealousy towards my dad and it exploded very publicly.

According to my dad it was like something out of a very bad slapstick comedy show.

Both of them now admit doing things that they can, and should, hang their heads in shame over. Each of them cheated during their repeated separations and my mum would even taunt my dad during arguments that I wasn't his son. It was a very toxic relationship.

By the time I was little more than two years old, any affection and trust that once existed between them had been completely destroyed. Their marriage and any pretence of a 'normal' family life for me was over. They divorced in 1985.

7
A new start

Over the next year both my mum and dad formed relationships with new partners and began to move on with their
lives.

My dad met Margaret, who was to become his second
wife and my stepmother, and settled down into the kind of
stable relationship he had been looking for all along but
until now had been too young and immature to realise.

Regretfully my mum wasn't so lucky in love. Life as a
single parent, especially for a woman with two boys, is never
easy and most of the men she attracted were, quite frankly,
no good for her or us.

After the divorce my dad tried to maintain a relationship
with Craig and me. We would visit him and Margaret on a
regular basis to give my mum a much-needed break.

During one of our visits my dad took Craig and me to get
a treat from the ice cream man. Like a lot of areas in Scotland
back then there used to be vans that travelled around almost
every residential street in towns selling sweets, pop, other
confectionary and, in some cases, stolen goods such as ciga-
rettes. It was even strongly rumoured that some of the vans
were dealing drugs although, to the best of my knowledge,
that has never been confirmed by the police or anyone else.

Glasgow was notorious back in the 1980s for turf wars
between rival criminal gangs trying to wrestle control of the
routes used by the ice cream vans that provided a vital service to many of the schemes outwith the city centre.

When Glasgow's most infamous slums were demolished in
the 1970s thousands of families were given new homes in major
purpose-built housing estates. Schemes such as Drumchapel,
Ruchazie, Easterhouse, Barlarnock, Garthanlock and Carn-
tyne became notorious as poverty-stricken, disaffected youths
deprived of hope and opportunities formed territorial gangs.

Anti-social behaviour was rife and many of the less
legitimate ice cream van operators would sometimes pay

youngsters to attack rival vans and smash them up. It all came to a head in 1984 when six members of the Doyle family were murdered in an arson attack on their home. The oldest son of the family, 18-year-old Andrew Doyle had been the main target of the attack because he had refused to sell drugs or let criminals take over his ice cream route.

The resulting public outcry resulted in a major police operation and a legal battle that lasted more than 20 years. Two men, local hard man TC Campbell and petty criminal Joe Steele, were jailed for the murders only to have their convictions later quashed and their prosecution described as one of the greatest miscarriages of justice in Scottish legal history. To this day the real killers have never been brought to justice.

Thankfully there was nothing criminal surrounding our trip to the ice cream van that day. Craig just wanted some Irn Bru, a fizzy soft drink peculiar to Scotland. Indeed, it's so popular here that while Coca-Cola is the top-selling soft drink almost everywhere else in the world, it is second to Irn Bru in Scotland.

In those days the drink was predominantly sold in glass bottles and Craig insisted on carrying the purchase himself. On the way back, he tripped and dropped the bottle. The glass shattered on the ground and Craig fell flat on his stomach on the broken shards, resulting in a deep cut to his abdomen.

The next day my dad went out fishing – he actually holds an international cap for representing Scotland in the world fishing championships. While he was out he left us in the care of his Aunt Betty. She regularly looked after us if he had to go to work during one of our visits.

As she was helping Craig get dressed Betty noticed the gash on Craig's body and her imagination ran wild. Not knowing about the incident, and without consulting my dad, she impulsively contacted Social Services and reported a case of 'potential abuse'. She thought the wound looked as though it might have been caused by the tip of a hot iron.

The Social Services child protection people didn't waste much time. They immediately came, inspected Craig's wound, and admitted both of us into protective care.

I vividly remember crying my eyes out when they took us away. I was hysterical and hanging onto the door frame as they tried to carry me out of the house. They had to prize my fingers away from the woodwork and I continued to struggle like mad as they put me in the car. I was screaming for my mum, kicking the back of the seats, the windows and the door of the car in a desperate attempt to escape.

That one single action had huge repercussions. Not only did it result in both Craig and me being taken away from my mum for a considerable period of time, it also shattered the already fragile relationship my mother and father had after splitting up.

We were put with a foster family for a while as my parents fought to get us returned. I don't remember too much about that time except that during the separation I picked up a strange habit of banging my head against walls in frustration and would often lash out at people in rage. I began biting anyone who I felt threatened by or who went near my mother. It was a trait I kept up until after I started school. In fact, a few of my early school reports from primary make mention of my being aggressive.

Luckily Craig and I were kept together. As my older brother he was the one person I felt safe with. I relied on his protection and clung to him like a limpet.

When my dad returned from his fishing trip and found out what had happened he had gone ballistic. He spent weeks on the phone, knocking on doors and setting up meetings with anybody who he thought could help get us back.

He even sat down with my mother and agreed the welfare of Craig and me was more important than their petty squabbles. He offered to give up any claims for custody if we were sent back to our mum. He willingly told the authorities that she was best placed to look after us.

It was a hard thing for my dad to do. Although his relationship with Margaret was still quite new she had been prepared to take us on as her own. When my dad went in front of the Children's Panel to argue the best thing for us was to go back to our mother, Margaret was devastated. She cried as if she had lost her own children. She had even given up her job as the manageress of a supermarket to look after us.

Thankfully the experts agreed and after about nine months Craig and I went home to live with my mum who had decided that a new start was required. That's when we moved from Govanhill to Rutherglen.

8

A sense of freedom

Our new home, a two-bedroom flat on the first floor of a refurbished red sandstone tenement building overlooking the main railway line from Glasgow to London, was a breath of fresh air.

It was only about two miles away from Govanhill but it might as well have been 100 as far as we were concerned. There used to be a swing park across the road from the flats and plenty of waste ground, with a derelict former toilet roll factory where a lot of the old alcoholics would congregate. We would go there to explore despite the place being awash with litter, empty beer cans, bottles, illegally dumped waste and discarded needles. The syringes left by drug addicts were a major problem, especially considering the fear of HIV and AIDS that dominated the news at that time. Fortunately I never heard of anyone getting hurt by a needle but I did stand on a rusty nail once and had to have a tetanus jag.

At the back of the park there was a steep hill which led down to the railway lines and we would often find ourselves down by the tracks when someone kicked the ball over the fence. Some of the kids would play dares to see who would run across the lines and back before a train came.

Being a dead-end street with no through traffic the area was a paradise for kids like us as we could enjoy a sense of freedom we had never experienced before.

I'm not sure all the neighbours really appreciated us moving in to their nice community though. We were the kids from the scheme and there were a lot of rules we hadn't been used to. There were certain places we couldn't play, like the back yard, and hanging about on the landing or hallway with pals was certainly frowned upon.

My mum told us we had been allocated the flat by the council as part of a house swap arrangement with the previous woman occupant who was looking to move to escape domestic abuse. However, in hindsight I think it was probably the other way around. I think one of the reasons she managed to get us back from being in care was to agree to move away and start a new life in a safer area.

But it didn't take long for my mum to fall into another bad relationship. I'm sure her choice of boyfriends definitely didn't help endear us to our new neighbours. While Dad had found some stability, my mum only seemed to attract heavy drinkers, bullies and chancers. Nice guys who turned up at our house didn't seem to last long.

I have never understood why she was attracted to such awful men. She certainly deserved so much better. Maybe it was a lack of self-confidence on her part but, at times, she seemed to enjoy flaunting such 'dangerous' relationships in front of my father.

One guy in particular was bad news for all of us. He was another wannabe hard man from Govanhill who liked to take a drink, or several. Unfortunately, the drink would usually end up taking him and he was an ugly drunk. He and my mother would have blazing rows which regularly resulted in some serious domestic violence. Craig and I would hide in our bedroom. We were terrified of him. No child should have to witness his mother with her face bruised and bloody, a broken nose or black eyes.

I have very vivid memories of coming out of my room one morning, after a particularly vicious fight between them the night before, and there were clumps of my mum's hair lying on the table and floor that he had ripped from her head.

Their relationship lasted on and off for several years but it never got any better. Why she kept taking him back is beyond me and I'm not sure she even knows why.

During one of their many break-ups, she did date one gentle guy called Davey. He was a farmer and he used to drive us up to his farm to see the animals. I remember the car rides with great fondness as we would all listen to his cassettes of Kenny Rogers and sing along to the music. He was probably the most decent bloke she dated but my mum's violent lover, whom I called Thug, managed to scare him off.

One day I was looking out the window when I saw Davey reversing his car up the street at high speed because Thug was chasing after him with a hammer. Even though he wasn't with my mum at the time, Thug wouldn't let anyone else be with her and very soon he had wormed his way back into our lives.

Although my mum did her best to protect us, it wasn't always possible. One particular night, Thug was drunk and especially aggressive. He had started punching and knocking Mum about because of some perceived slight. She tried to get away and ran into the kitchen in a bid to put as much distance between them as she could. But Thug was in no mood to stop and charged in after her. In a desperate attempt to defend herself she picked up the nearest object she could reach, which just happened to be a knife, and stabbed Thug. Fortunately it wasn't a life-threatening injury but the police were called and my mother was arrested for assault. She ended up spending the weekend locked in a police cell while Thug was treated for a minor wound and allowed home to us. Mum was finally released without charge after Thug refused to make a statement to the police, but he never let her forget that he had 'saved' her from prosecution.

Sometimes Craig and I would get hurt in the madness when the two of them were fighting and we got flung out of the way, although on occasion he could turn his anger on us too.

I remember one time when there wasn't much money going about and I was into sticker books at the time. There was a £1 note lying on the coffee table and I took it and put it in my room. I was planning to buy four packs of football stickers, or something like that.

Unfortunately Thug spotted it had disappeared and held this big investigation into the missing pound. He knew it was me or Craig and was determined to punish at least one of us. He decided it had to be Craig and started laying into him with his fists. To try and make the violence stop I 'found' the pound but Craig still got battered for it.

When Thug discovered it was me who had taken the money he almost seemed delighted as he switched his violent rage from Craig to me. I was hit with a leather belt so hard that the metal buckle caught me on the neck and left a mark. When I went into school the next day I knew if I told the teachers what had happened my mum would get into trouble so I claimed I'd hurt myself climbing over a wire fence in the play park. On the plus side, I never stole anything ever again. It was a very big moment in my life.

Looking back, living in such an atmosphere was an education in acting that was to prove very useful for my future. As a matter of self-preservation, I quickly learned how to read Thug's mood in the same way I have since learned to read an audience.

There were numerous occasions when Mum, Craig and I would be sitting watching television and we would hear the buzzer to the main door. There was a security latch on the access to the building and anyone who didn't have a key, or didn't want to use one, would have to ring the bell of the flat they intended to visit to be let in. The buzzer would go once, then again and again and again.

Instinctively we all knew who it was. We would then listen intently, with our hearts in our mouths and our stomachs churning, as Thug managed to gain entrance to the block and drunkenly staggered up the communal stairs to the flat.

Almost immediately the mood in the room would have changed from lighthearted and fun-loving to one of fear and trepidation. As soon as we heard him trying to get in we knew what we had to do.

Thug was often so drunk he couldn't get the key into the lock and my mum would have to rush and let him into the flat. She would immediately start blaming the mechanism and say things like 'that blasted lock is no use, the key never fits first time'. She would babble on about anything to try and keep him calm.

Craig and I would instantly pretend to be delighted to see him. We'd try and make him feel important and comfortable while my mum ran to the bathroom to put on some make-up to please 'her man' and try to 'look nice' for him. Without a single word being spoken between us we all knew we had to create a positive environment so he didn't get mad and start laying into one of us.

We would sit in fear for what seemed like hours listening to his drunken ramblings as we watched for any tell-tale signs that he was about to kick off. A glint in his eye, a sudden sneer or a variation of tone in his voice were all signals we had learned would indicate a split-second change in his frame of mind.

The slightest thing could set him off. If we were too slow to do something he wanted, if we laughed when we shouldn't or didn't laugh when we should he could get violent. I had learned the hard way to not show any outward signs of panic but inside I would be trembling. Like a wild animal he could smell fear and would pounce on it.

Often when Thug got really angry my mum would send us running upstairs to our neighbour, Mrs Brown, for help. She was the only person in our block with a telephone. On more than one occasion I had to scramble out of bed late at night, dressed only in my boxer shorts or pyjamas, and escape to her flat. I would bang on her door and Mrs Brown would find me trembling and gasping for breath on the front step as I tearfully begged her to call the police. She would take me in, sit me in an armchair with a blanket and give me a drink and a biscuit until either the police arrived or things calmed down by themselves.

What made it worse for me was I daren't tell anyone outside the home other than Mrs Brown, and I didn't even tell her everything. I was terrified Craig and I would get taken away and put into care again.

I used to resent having to go to school, after being up until 4am in the morning with the police at the door following some violent row. The teachers would want to know why I hadn't done my homework and I couldn't tell them the truth. I felt I had to bottle it up or risk losing my mum. It wasn't the teachers' fault but I still begrudged them for giving me a difficult time for not trying harder with my studies.

However, even now, decades later, those moments when he terrorised us are hard to think about, although I've learned to put them to good use. Whenever I'm asked to do an emotional scene or one that requires me to show fear or anger I think about those days and it does the trick every time.

What makes it especially painful is that it was because of Thug that my father stopped coming to see us. Initially, after the divorce, he would visit us every two or three weeks, bring presents and send cards and gifts on special occasions.

Thug tried to abuse my dad's relationship with us by demanding more and more money for our support. One day he showed up at my father's workplace with Craig and me in the pushchair. He had been drinking and claimed he wanted money to buy shoes for us. He was really after some cash to buy more alcohol and my dad knew it. He had seen similar behaviour when he was a child and refused point blank.

Instead of handing over money my dad said he would take us shopping or give my mum the cash. Thug immediately got aggressive. It was a stunt he pulled more than once, suddenly appearing at my dad's house or the home of one of his relatives.

Around this time my half-sister Leanne had just been born and my dad began to worry Thug would start causing trouble for his new family, and that innocent people were going to get hurt.

The final straw was when my dad came to visit, sometime around my birthday, to give Craig and me some money. Thug was at the flat and wanted him to hand the money over to him. My dad very wisely refused because he thought we would never see it. Thug quickly became aggressive and threatened to shoot my dad with a crossbow. That was the end. My dad never came back to visit and I didn't see him again for more than 20 years.

9
DNA test

Not seeing my dad hurt very much. At weekends I would sit for hours looking out of the window, watching the corner of the street willing him to suddenly appear.

I didn't understand why he had stopped coming around so I would do daft things in the hope of changing reality. In the same way some sports people have superstitions about which sock they put on first I would sit in exactly the same position I had been in when he last visited. I hoped I would be able to make him magically materialise or somehow set in motion a series of events that would result in a visit. Why is there never a fairy godmother or grateful leprechaun when you need one? I was obsessed with trying to get a wish from some spiritual being.

Whenever we went on the bus through the Clyde tunnel, a 2,500ft long roadway that goes under the river linking the north and south sides of Glasgow, I would hold my breath. I had this funny idea that if I could stop breathing until we got out the other side I would get a wish and all I wanted was for my dad to visit. It never worked!

After reconnecting with my father as an adult I have since learned his reasons for staying away and I can honestly say I don't blame him. He had been through so much growing up and needed to break the cycle.

My dad had found happiness with Margaret and had a new family. He wasn't prepared to put them at risk. I believe him when he says he has enormous regrets about keeping his distance from Craig and me.

Unfortunately my mother didn't, and still doesn't, agree with his reasoning. She felt very bitter about his walking away and her anger sometimes got the better of her.

Things came to a head sometime around 1986 or 1987 when he received a letter from the Department of Health and Social Security (DHSS) ordering him to make regular child support payments to my mother.

My dad, who was unemployed at the time – one of the few occasions in his life when he wasn't working – challenged the order because of my mother's previous claims that I wasn't his biological son. In view of the secret he had been carrying around about his own parentage I'm not surprised he asked for a DNA test.

Obviously, at the time I knew nothing of this but I do recall having to go to the doctor for a blood sample to be taken. I was told it was needed because of the constant earaches I experienced after going swimming. From an early age I had suffered from a perforated eardrum but was told it couldn't be fixed until I was an adult. The blood test was to see if I would be deaf like my grandad and I accepted all this without question.

When I was older I went to a doctor and repeated what I'd been told only to find out it was complete nonsense. I could have had the operation anytime. That's when I realised the blood had been taken for a DNA profile. As it turned out the test confirmed beyond any doubt I was my father's son, much to his relief.

However, my mother's bad taste in men and my dad's desire to avoid bringing trouble to his new family meant that while he was prepared to pay monthly child support for Craig and me he still kept away from our door.

On more than one occasion Thug turned up at my father's workplace, the home in Newton Means he shared with Margaret and his new family, and the homes of his friends and other family members, demanding money he claimed he was owed for 'bringing up' his sons. My dad was worried that other people were going to get hurt.

Even after Mum's relationship with Thug finished she took up with another hard man, a guy from Castlemilk. Although he died a few years ago, at the time he was seeing my mum, was notorious in the area for being a 'bit of a nutter'. My half-sister Leanne was born around then and Margaret was pregnant with another of my sisters, Debbie. My father was terrified that my mum's lifestyle and choice of partners would continue to bring trouble to the door of his new family.

Newton Mearns, although only about ten miles from where we lived in Rutherglen, is an affluent and genteel, middle-class suburb of Glasgow that is full of two-car families in a range of houses complete with their own front doors and gardens. My dad moved there because he thought his and Margaret's kids would be safer and get better schooling away from the negative influences of the schemes that he had grown up among.

Things were further complicated later on when Margaret and their four kids – my sisters Leanne, Debbie, Lindsay and brother Steven – became Jehovah's Witnesses.

Margaret lost both of her parents within weeks of each other and it was tough time for her. She was looking for answers and found comfort from the Jehovah's Witnesses. It worked for her and she ended up getting baptised into the faith. Then she got her brother and his family into it. Leanne married Stuart, another Witness from Kirkintilloch, and then Debbie got involved with the church and married Jonathan. Although not a member of the faith my dad had little choice but to live the life. Jehovah's Witnesses don't celebrate birthdays, Christmas or Easter, which made things even more difficult. He felt he couldn't be Santa in one house and not the other. He couldn't buy Craig and me birthday presents and not the other children. It was therefore easier not to buy anybody anything so in the end we saw him less and drifted even further apart.

I thought then that he didn't care about us. I now know differently. It's clear his own childhood and his remorse over Craig and me caused him serious emotional turmoil. He felt guilty about spending too much time with his new family when he didn't see us so he threw himself into work and wasn't as good a dad as he wanted to be to any of his children. The actions and regrets which stemmed from one area of his life prevented him from fully enjoying another.

10

My first time treading the boards

Aside from not seeing my dad, and the minor moments of terror inflicted by the likes of Thug and a couple of my mother's later boyfriends, I've always felt my childhood was a reasonably good one. But then I never knew anything different.

Mum, Craig and I were a pretty close-knit team. We looked out for each other. Money was always in short supply but there was a lot of laughter and we did okay. I don't ever remember going hungry for any real length of time or not having clothes to wear, although we did only get new stuff twice a year – birthdays and Christmas.

Even now, as an adult I tend to do most of my clothes shopping in June, around my birthday, and December, because those were the two times I was ever given money to spend as a kid and the habit has stuck with me.

When we were youngsters Craig and I would get the same playthings. If one of us got a toy truck the other got the same. Craig would often break his and my mum would give him mine just to keep the peace. I guess she figured that being two years younger I wouldn't realise. That's one of the few things I remember my mum and granny arguing about. Sadie used to warn my mother that she would regret it when I was old enough to understand what was happening and that she was teaching Craig it was ok to mistreat his toys because he would just be given another one – mine!

It was tough as a one-parent family, especially in the 1980s when there were more than three million people unemployed in the UK. However, my mum was never out of work. At one time she had five different jobs on the go at once, working up to 16 hours a day, to make sure my brother and I never went without the basic necessities of food, clothing and a roof over our heads. Hard work has never been something my family has been afraid of. Even my granny, Sadie, who was a widow for 30 years after my granddad died, had multiple jobs. She worked as a carer for a while during the day and sold pies at Hampden football stadium on match days.

Occasionally there would be some money left over for treats, such as a toy or a day out and those moments were magical. They also helped me to understand the value of money and not to take life's little luxuries for granted.

We lived on a street where most kids had a mum and dad who worked and they could afford the latest toys, trendiest clothes and to go on school trips. My mum always made sure we never went without or missed out on too much. She would regularly leave home early in the morning before Craig and I were awake. She would creep into our bedroom, set the alarm clock in time for us to get up and ready for school and then quietly slip out the flat and go off to an early cleaning job.

After spending all morning cleaning other people's houses she would then waitress at a local pub at lunchtime, clean the local shopping arcade in the early evenings and work as a barmaid at night. She rarely got home until after midnight when Craig and I were already asleep.

I used to go the arcade to meet her after school and if one of the other cleaners didn't turn up for their shift I would be given a broom and get paid £1 for an hour of sweeping, cleaning the seats or emptying the ashtrays.

Of course, Mum working so much meant Craig and I were pretty much latch-key kids left to our own devices. We were almost always out with the neighbourhood gang and didn't spend much time in the house, unless it was really cold or raining. Among our friends we always seem to be first out in the street and the last to go in. Mum working so many jobs meant we never had to go home for dinner like the others. She would just leave some change and tell us to buy some chips or something.

The children from our street did everything together. We would get shopping trolleys from the local supermarkets and race each other up and down the streets. In winter we would pinch traffic cones and squash them down to use as sledges when there was snow.

Sometimes a big group of us would go to the cinema. We'd club together some money for three or four of the gang to pay to get in and then they would open the fire escape doors to let the rest of us in for free.

Our other money-saving dodge, especially on cold days, was to ride the number 90 bus around Glasgow. Some of the boys would pay to get on the bus at one stop and when it pulled up further down the road they would open the back window for the others to climb on out of sight of the driver. I only remember it backfiring once. Craig was one of the boys who had skipped on the bus fare, as he had bought crisps and juice with his money. But for some reason there was a change of driver at Govan who decided to check everyone's tickets. Craig was quickly thrown off the bus and left stranded miles from home without any money. I was one of the younger boys in the group that day and remember being really upset that I'd lost my brother. Fortunately Craig had the presence of mind to approach a policeman and spun some story about losing his money. They gave him enough change for the next bus home.

Overall I think I enjoyed a pretty free-spirited childhood in many ways, even though Craig and I had to behave ourselves much more than our friends. We were repeatedly warned by Mum to never get involved in anything that brought the police or authorities to our door.

It was drummed into us that because she was a single mum and didn't have anyone to look after us we'd have to fend for ourselves a lot, but nobody was allowed to find out. If we misbehaved or let the neighbours know we were in the house on our own she wouldn't be able to go to work, and if she couldn't work we wouldn't have any money. And Social Services could even get involved.

She put the fear of God into me. If any of my pals started doing something that could lead to trouble with the police I would always have an excuse ready, such as needing to go to the toilet or run an errand. I felt a bit like I was chickening out but there was no way on earth I was ever going to risk being taken away from my mum and put into care again.

Having to keep our home life something of a secret forged an even closer bond between Craig and me. As you'd expect from brothers, we would sometimes fight and tear lumps out of each other, usually over silly things. However, we would always stick together against anyone from outside the family.

Occasionally I think my overactive imagination or desire to perform embarrassed him. More than once he would complain to my mum that my antics were a complete riddy – a good Scots word meaning embarrassment – as they say in Glasgow.

Halloween, especially, must have been one of those mortifying occasions for Craig as I would always insist upon dressing up and going guising. Before the term 'trick or treat' was imported from America in recent years, children in Scotland would dress up in costumes and go guising or galoshin' to neighbouring houses. The idea stems from an ancient custom that children in disguise would blend in with spirits walking the earth on All Hallow's Eve. Homeowners would provide any entity that knocked on their door an offering of some kind to ward off evil.

Over the years the custom has evolved so guisers would only receive a treat if they performed a song, dance or told a joke first. That's the bit I loved.

As a youngster I was quite a fan of the Scottish singer Andy Stewart. I would dress up in an old schoolgirl's tartan skirt, which my mum had found somewhere and turned into a makeshift kilt for me. At the age of six I would love going to the neighbours' houses and singing Andy Stewart's 'Donald Where's Yer Troosers' and a 'Bonnie wee lass called Jeannie McColl'.

Despite his obvious unease at my desire for the spotlight Craig was a protective big brother, perhaps because of the bond we had forged to survive what was happening at home. He certainly made things easier for me when I started at Burgh Primary School.

I remember my first day going into the primary one class to meet my teacher, Mrs MacDonald. I did not want to go as I was frightened of being separated from my mum again. I was kicking, screaming and holding on to my mum for dear life. Eventually I was prized away and within a short time had settled down.

I was always known as Kyle's little brother at school so all the bullies left me alone because they knew he would quickly sort out anyone who tried to give me a hard time. Happily, he didn't have to step in very often as Burgh school was quite a friendly wee place. It's where I first got a taste of the acting bug when I was given the highly important role of a shepherd in the school nativity performance at the Rutherglen Parish Church.

I loved my first time treading the boards and was delighted the following Christmas when I was cast in the chorus of the school's production of *Cinderella*. I had wanted to play Prince Charming but that was given to another boy in my class, Craig Kelly.

Craig was really nice kid and very popular with the rest of the class, especially the girls as he was good looking. He had the perfect family, a great mum and dad, and everything going for him.

Unfortunately, as has happened far too often in Glasgow, he never got a chance to realise his full potential. He was stabbed to death in a senseless brawl aged just 25 in 2009.

It was one of those needless tragedies that have blighted so many lives over the years. Craig and another man, David Kingsman, had some kind of ongoing rivalry and on 17 March 2009 it all came to a head.

After a series of on and off confrontations throughout the day both men got into a fight at a gathering in a flat in Rutherglen in which Craig is said to have hit Kingsman with a bottle. He retaliated by killing Craig with a single stab wound to the chest. Kingsman was jailed for six years after admitting culpable homicide, the Scottish equivalent of manslaughter.

Craig's was the first funeral I ever attended and a lot of people from my school years were there. Everybody had kind stories to tell about him, including his brilliant performance as a six-year-old Prince Charming.

It was a very emotional experience for me, not least because if it hadn't been for him I might have been killed, or at least seriously injured, as a result of gang violence, several years before.

11

No Mean City

Gang culture was endemic in Glasgow when I was growing up, especially in some of the less affluent areas of the city. Like a bad smell you get used to, but are constantly aware of, there was often a hint of menace in the air. At the back of your mind there was always a sense of trepidation that even the silliest of confrontations could suddenly turn violent or even deadly.

Where do you come from? What school did you go to? Who do you fancy for the match on Saturday? These were frequent types of questions often asked by complete strangers if you found yourself standing at a bus stop or drinking beer in a pub situated outside your usual stomping grounds. Far from being innocuous small talk, as these seemingly innocent enquires may seem to somebody from outside Glasgow or the West of Scotland, the answers could be critical to your safety. They were a method of sussing out your religion, soccer allegiance and neighbourhood. If the questioner didn't like the answers you gave it could lead to a beating, or at least a fear-inducing, adrenaline-fuelled chase through the streets of the city.

Gangs have been associated with Glasgow since the late 19th century.

If you ever visit the old Britannia Panopticon theatre in the Trongate, the Victorian Music Hall where comedian Stan Laurel made his stage debut, there is graffiti carved into the woodwork of the balcony that references the rival Tongs and San Toys, gangs notorious on the streets of the city at the time, and for a good number of years since.

For much of the 19th and 20th century Glasgow was an industrial city that attracted people from all corners of Scotland, Ireland and elsewhere. There was a lot of poverty, overcrowding and squalor. Life was hard for many people and self-preservation was the name of the game. This led to a lot of men, most of them young but by no means all, forming cliques or gangs to 'protect' their street, block or district from 'outsiders'.

Some of these gangs became organised criminal enterprises involved in thievery, protection rackets, extortion, robbery and anything else that created a little money. They had little respect for the law or fear of the police.

Gangs such as the Penny Mob started in the East End of Glasgow and had their own dress style and rules – real-life Peaky Blinders in a way. They got their name by charging members a penny subscription which went towards paying any court fines or bailing out arrested associates.

Other crews such as the Redskins got their name from the facial scars most of them carried proudly and which gave their skin a reddish hue. There were also the Billy Boys, the San Toys, the Gold Dust Gang, the Mealy Boys, the Tim Malloys, the Bloodhound Flying Corps, the McGlynn Push, the Baltic Fleet, the Cumbie, the Shamrock, the Kelly Boys, the Hi-Hi's, the Black Hand and many more. They were all fiercely competitive, extremely territorial and very violent.

It was not uncommon for mass brawls to break out in the street or organised 'rumbles' to be held at Glasgow Green where rival mobs would attack each other with bricks, bottles, razors, knives, machetes, swords or weighted clubs. Confrontations were usually over quickly but they were savage and very bloody.

Back in the 1920s gangs armed with razors fought pitched battles in the streets, giving inspiration to the 1935 book by Alexander MacArthur and H Kingsley Long. Its title *No Mean City* became a byword for Glasgow and, rightly or wrongly, was for many years considered an accurate account of life in Scotland's largest metropolis.

In 1931 Percy Sillitoe was appointed Chief Constable of the City of Glasgow Police. A no nonsense copper he decided to fight fire with fire and recruited a lot of big, brawny

Highlanders to the force to take on the gangs. Between 1931 and 1943 he managed to break the stranglehold that a lot of the gangs had over parts of the city.

He was also influential in replacing old corner police telephone boxes with wireless radios for police cars and, most famously, introducing the Sillitoe tartan. More commonly recognised as the band of black and white diced pattern ribbon worn around police caps, it was brought in so officers could be more easily distinguished from members of other emergency services, such as the ambulance crews and firefighters of the day. The idea proved such a success it has since been adopted by police in many other countries, including Australia, New Zealand and some law enforcement departments in the USA, most notably Chicago and Pittsburgh.

However, despite the efforts of Sillitoe and countless initiatives over the last 90-plus years gang culture remains ingrained in Glasgow life and continues to this day.

As a young boy I remember it was common to see men, both young and old, with severe facial wounds caused by razors or bottles. Often referred to as a 'Glasgow smile', many of these battle scars were worn as a badge of pride among some sections of the community.

At one time, as recently as the early 2000s, doctors in Glasgow had to regularly deal with some of the worst facial wounds seen anywhere in the world.

Sometimes individual members of rival gangs would be selected to settle a dispute in what was called 'a square go' – a bare-knuckle fight between two champions who would slug it out for the 'honour' of their crew. However, as often as not, many of these 'fair fights' turned into mass brawls.

Poverty has always been a major contributor to the allure of gang life and Glasgow has had a lot of it over the years.

Shortly after World War One returning troops found the promise they were given of a home fit for heroes was a myth and a shortage of employment fuelled gang membership. It was the same in the Depression of the 1930s, during the decline of the city's industrial powerhouse in the 1960s and 1970s, and the recessions of the 1980s and 1990s.

There have been numerous initiatives over the years to try and combat the culture of violence with both the carrot and stick being used, to varying degrees of success.

In the 1960s the then police commissioner introduced Group Disorder Vehicles, which were really rapid response teams, made up of a police sergeant and several of the biggest bobbies they could find, to crack down on gang violence whenever and wherever it erupted in the city. They became known on the streets as The Untouchables, named after the US television series of the same name starring Robert Stack as Elliott Ness. For some reason the TV show was particularly popular in Glasgow at the time and the name stuck, in the same way today that youngsters use the American term Feds as a slang term for police.

In addition to the Untouchables the authorities also tried tougher prison sentences for violent crime, police amnesties to encourage the surrender of weapons and investment in youth facilities – all of which have had assorted results.

Famously, in the late 1960s, the singer and actor Frankie Vaughan visited Easterhouse, one of the worst areas for youth violence in Glasgow at the time. He managed to negotiate a truce between rival gangs and raised thousands of pounds to create clubs, youth centres and activities to keep teenagers out of trouble. It was a fantastic effort and it worked, for a while.

By the time I was a teenager in the late nineties and early noughties violence and gang culture was again rife throughout parts of the city which, according to the experts, had the highest number of street gangs in the UK.

Around the time I was entering my teens it was estimated there were some 170 gangs or more in Glasgow, which for a city with a population of less than 600,000 is a lot.

It came as no surprise when Glasgow was named the murder capital of Western Europe by the United Nations' crime research institute. It claimed Scots were nearly three times more likely to be victims of violent assaults than people living in the United States. That's a sobering thought, considering the US has a population of almost 330 million – 550 times the number of people in Glasgow.

And more than 50 per cent of all knives confiscated by the police in Scotland were seized in Glasgow where stabbings accounted for half of all murders.

Rivalry between street gangs was intense and they guarded their turf viciously. I remember Craig used to have to sneak up to his then-girlfriend's house in the adjoining area of Blairbeth, a small housing estate only a short distance from where we lived. In order to avoid trouble from the lads in that area, who would chase him on sight for being from another hood, he would have to get a taxi when he had money or sneak up through the bushes and take a long way round to come in at the back of the estate without being spotted. I know it might seem ridiculous to anyone who has never experienced it but these dangers were, and remain, real for thousands of people.

I realise now just how lucky I was not to get caught up in that world, although at times it was a pretty close-run thing. There was always a lot of peer pressure to get involved with a gang, especially if you lived in certain parts of the city where if you didn't align yourself with a crew you were in danger of being attacked by all sides.

I was always careful to try and not get involved in anything which might bring the police to our home. My mum made it very clear to us that we could end up in care again and I was not going to let that happen.

However, one summer evening I found myself in the thick of a pitched battle and it was an experience I wouldn't want to repeat.

My mum had gone for a rare night out with some of the women from her job at the supermarket and Craig had a girlfriend round at our house.

Mum had been very reluctant to go but our neighbour, Evelyn, said it would be okay as she would pop in and out to keep an eye on me and Craig.

Once Mum had gone, Evelyn had checked in on us and Craig was occupied in the living room with his girlfriend, I was left to my own devices. It was then I saw an opportunity for a taste of freedom. While everyone thought I was in my bedroom I sneaked out of the flat and went down the road to flirt with some of the girls from the neighbourhood.

Unbeknownst to me a few of the local lads from our street had got into a feud with a rival group from a nearby scheme. There was a fight arranged and both sides had decided to meet up at the local park, which we all called the Fighting Field, to sort things out once and for all.

I wasn't interested in getting involved, I'd much preferred to spend my time talking to girls rather than scrapping. But, just as I felt I was getting somewhere chatting up a girl called Aileen one of the lads from the street, Peter, turned up looking for reinforcements. The rival gang had arrived in larger numbers than expected and our side needed everybody they could get.

I tried to stay out of it but Peter piled on the pressure, especially in front of Aileen. He told me not to be a 'shitebag' and get down there to help the local lads against the Blairbeth boys.

The more I tried to ignore his cajoling the greater the peer pressure he piled on and, not wanting to look like a coward in front of Aileen, I eventually, and reluctantly, agreed.

However, my timing could not have been worse. I took off at speed down to the park and as I turned a corner I found myself running in the wrong direction. Much to my horror the tide of battle had turned and my side was in full retreat with the bloodthirsty Blairbeth crew hot on their heels. I almost got trampled in the stampede but just managed to get out of the way.

I saw a bottle laying on the ground so I picked it up and threw it at the attackers, turned on my toes and started running for my life with the rest of my pals.

Unfortunately the Blairbeth boys were older, bigger and faster. I was only 14 and they must have been about 18 or 19 years old and capable of running a lot quicker than me. They were also armed to the teeth with bottles, bats and knives.

Sensing I was in danger of being caught I threw myself on the ground and they ran right over me in pursuit of my pals. As soon as they disappeared I immediately sprang to my feet and tore off full pelt in the opposite direction – only to run smack into the middle of a second wave of Blairbeth boys who set about me like a pack of savage dogs.

Unable to defend myself I curled up into a ball as they kicked, punched and lashed out at me with belts, buckles, bottles and an array of other makeshift weapons.

My heart was beating so fast I thought it would burst. I couldn't scream but remember feeling terrified that this was it, that they were going to kill me.

Luckily two lassies saw what was happening and tried to break up the assault. They stood with my head between their feet in an attempt to stop the bigger boys kicking or stamping on my face and cracking my skull.

The beating probably lasted only a few seconds but felt like an eternity. It was as if my mind had applied the brakes to the very passage of time and turned everything into a slow-motion, frame-by-frame edit of reality. I could almost see, as well as feel, each individual punch, kick or battering as it made contact with my body.

As soon as the Blairbeth boys got bored they took off in search of another victim and left me lying in a pool of blood, bruised and gasping for breath.

I don't know how long I stayed on the ground but it was a real struggle to get up. My arms, hands and legs were covered in deep gashes and scratches. I could hardly see as my face was smeared with blood and it was dripping into my eyes. My nose and lips were bleeding profusely, part of my ear was hanging off, there were several deep cuts to the side and back of my head and my leg hurt so much I thought my knee had been dislocated.

I also felt betrayed. I would never have left any of my friends like they had left me. The only one to come back and help was Craig Kelly, the Pantomime Prince Charming who was to die a few years later in a needless act of violence. He helped to carry me home.

I remember staggering into the flat where my brother and his girlfriend were sitting on the sofa watching television. The look of shock on their faces as I stumbled through the door covered in blood and pleading with them, 'Don't tell Ma', will stay with me forever.

Unfortunately I was in such a mess there was no hiding it. They had to call an ambulance and I was taken to Victoria Infirmary hospital while Evelyn, our neighbour who had agreed to keep an eye on us, had to phone the hotel where my mum's party was being held to tell her what had happened.

By the time my mum got to the hospital, doctors had sewn back part of my ear. A small piece of soft tissue had been severed by a broken bottle and left hanging by a thread. They had also stitched the wounds to my head, bandaged my knee and given me a set of crutches.

For the next few days I was the talk of the steamie. For those who weren't brought up in Glasgow, the steamie was the name given to the public washhouses that could be found in almost every community where the local women would do their laundry. Inevitably such places were always a centre for gossip.

As with most rumours that get elaborated with each repetition, dramatic tales abounded around the local community that I'd been almost decapitated. Some people heard I had been left on a life-support machine, others that my ear had been completely severed while a few were even told I had been completely scalped by a Blairbeth savage, just like we used to see in cowboy movies.

My poor mum had to cope with a string of local youngsters coming to the door each day asking to see my injuries or find out what happened and whether I knew who did it. They just wanted the gory details to feed the local gossip and she sent them all away with a flea in their ear. Only one boy, Wullie Darroch, came to ask if I was okay and if I needed anything. It taught me a valuable lesson about human nature and the differences between false friends and genuine acts of kindness.

I pretty much stopped hanging around the park with big crowds of kids after that. I found I would rather just have a few close mates round to the flat as I'd discovered that in friendship, as with a lot of things in life, quality is almost always better than quantity.

Today, there are still lots of gangs in Glasgow, albeit with more modern names ending in the likes of toi, tong, young team, sqwad and possie.

They are still driven by boredom, poverty and disillusionment and fuelled by drugs, alcohol and bravado but they are just as likely to be found trading insults or arranging fights on social media as they are standing on street corners.

However, things have improved in the last 15 years as a result of a dramatic change in approach to policing.

In 2005 the authorities set up the Violence Reduction Unit (VRU) to drive down knife crime. In combination with better targeted stop and search operations by police and tougher sentences from the courts for carrying knives the VRU began treating the problem as a public health issue.

Officers liaised with teachers, social workers, health staff and other bodies to identify and treat the root causes of the problem rather than just the symptoms of the disease.

The areas of the city with the worst gang problems are the poorest with the highest rates of addiction, despair, domestic abuse, teenage pregnancy and deprivation. The VRU started to engage with the gangs, brought in ex-offenders to talk to the youngsters, and offered an alternative lifestyle free from violence, drugs, alcohol and toxic masculinity.

The result has been a sustained long-term reduction in incidents which has saved countless lives. If only such a scheme had been around ten years earlier my brother Craig might not have been embroiled in an attempted murder case.

12

Sweet sixteen

For most people reaching the grand old age of 16 is a joyous occasion, a celebration akin to a rite of passage for most teenagers, in Scotland anyway.

It is the age a youngster can legally have sex, get married, leave school, move out of their parents' home, join the army, drive a moped, get a full-time job, and even buy a lottery ticket with the chance of becoming an overnight multi-millionaire.

But, it is also the point in life when a juvenile becomes an adult in the eyes of the Scottish courts system – with all the repercussions and consequences that such a landmark moment brings. My brother Craig's memorable day was certainly unforgettable, but for all the wrong reasons.

Tuesday 29 April 1997 was never going to be 'ordinary'. It was Craig's 16th birthday and the start of his adult life, with all the promise and opportunity that comes with reaching the age of consent and responsibility.

Almost from the moment we woke up in the morning there was an air of excitement in the flat. Mum and I wished Craig a happy birthday and I remember us talking about how we might celebrate as a family later that night, after we were home from school and Mum had finished work.

We weren't the only ones planning a surprise for Craig. A couple of weeks earlier, during the evening of Thursday 17 April, Craig and I had been hanging out at the park just a short distance from our home which, as I said previously, was known locally as The Fighting Field. We were just two of several dozen youngsters who regularly gathered there for something to do. Some came to chat up girls, others to play football and some, as the name of the location suggests, fight with rival gangs of boys from neighbouring schemes.

This relatively tiny recreation ground, situated in a kind of 'no-man's land' between several housing estates, was where individuals could sort out their differences in a fair fight or rival gangs could settle grudges for some perceived insult and indulge in mass brawls out of sheer boredom. It has been called 'The Fighting Field' for decades, almost from the moment the surrounding housing estates were built in the 1950s. It was well known as such by the police who would frequently patrol the area and show up to try and disperse groups of youngsters before any trouble started. They frequently failed.

On this particular evening I must have been especially irritating to my big brother and was obviously cramping his style in front of the girls as he told me to go home and chased me off the field. Looking back on that day I thank God that he did.

A short time after I left a few boys from the neighbouring estate, Toryglen, showed up at the field. They were members of the Toi gang and archrivals of the lads from my neighbourhood, Rutherglen, who were known simply as The Glen.

The police were quick off the mark and arrived to advise the rival groups to go home but almost as soon as the officers had left the youngsters gravitated back to the Fighting Field.

What exactly happened next remains somewhat unclear but what is known is that shortly after 10pm, William Gaddie, an 18-year-old apprentice stonemason from Toryglen, arrived at the field with some other lads from the Toi gang.

Somehow he became separated from his friends, after stopping to chat to a couple of girls, and was suddenly ambushed by members of The Glen.

It appears two of the Glen boys, both aged 17, spotted Gaddie and charged out of the bushes brandishing sticks as makeshift clubs. Before Gaddie had time to run he was tripped up, pushed to the ground and his attackers began kicking, stamping, punching and beating him with sticks, bottles and metal poles.

They were cheered on by five other members of the Glen gang, ranging in ages from 15 to 18, who surrounded the fallen Gaddie and were shouting, screaming and waving sticks as they encouraged the attack.

I don't know exactly how long the beating went on for but for Gaddie it must have seemed like an eternity. He was only saved after some members of his own gang showed up and chased off the Glen boys so they could carry away their injured friend, only to abandon him in the road when they heard police sirens homing in on the area.

Officers had been called by local residents alarmed by the sight of yet another running street battle outside their homes. When the cops arrived they found Gaddie lying unconscious on the ground.

It was immediately clear he had been very seriously injured. He was rushed to Southern General Hospital by ambulance where doctors found his skull had been fractured. A piece of bone had broken off and pierced his brain so he had to undergo an urgent operation. For a time it was touch and go whether he would survive.

Immediately following the attack detectives launched an attempted murder investigation and began tracing everyone who had been present on the field that night. I was among those interviewed but, as Craig had sent me home early, I couldn't tell them anything.

Unfortunately somebody must have given Craig's name. That's when a nightmare that was to last more than a year, and changed our family dynamic forever, began.

Craig had been only 15 years old when the incident happened and therefore could not be interviewed without a parent, responsible adult or solicitor present. But, when two dapper suited detectives showed up at our door on the evening of 29 April – 12 days after the incident – Craig was 16 years old. They knew it was his birthday and I am convinced they deliberately waited so they could get him alone.

After announcing they were carrying out an attempted murder investigation Craig was taken to the local police station to 'help with enquiries'.

I like to think that to some extent Craig and I were streetwise. We knew to try and keep out of trouble but I have to admit we were not so astute when it came to dealing with the police. Neither Craig nor I had ever been involved in any bother like this before and he didn't have a clue what to do.

Mum was still at work when the detectives showed up at our door and took Craig away but as soon as she found out she rushed down to the police station. Despite her demands to see Craig, and her protests that he needed representation, the cops refused to let her anywhere near my brother. They told her if Craig wanted a lawyer he could ask for one, but they certainly never told him that.

Unable to gain access or get a message to Craig Mum was left running around the outside of the station screaming at the top of her voice: 'Ask for a lawyer, Craig'. She was hoping that somehow he would hear her and at least request to see a solicitor, as he was legally entitled to do.

Unfortunately Craig didn't get the message and the police played the old good cop versus bad cop routine. They convinced him he didn't need any legal representation if he was innocent and suggested that bringing in a lawyer could make him look guilty. The police clearly knew, or at least strongly suspected, who was responsible. Craig was put under immense pressure, he wasn't allowed to rest or given any refreshments. He was just questioned, cajoled and threatened for hour after hour through the night. Eventually the police had to let Craig go but once word got out that

Craig was involved, he had to be careful wherever he went. He had to take different routes between school and home, and he was always watching his back.

As the pressure of the case mounted Craig went to live with our father in Newton Mearns. That was a big blow for my mum, especially when you know their history. She worried that he would somehow turn Craig against her.

To be fair, Craig didn't want to go either because he had not, and still hasn't, forgiven our dad for walking out on us when we were kids. Living with our father's new family was a desperate last-case scenario and a clear indication of just how scared we all were at what was happening.

Compared to Rutherglen, and its rows of tenement flats, bored teenagers roaming the streets and overcrowded bus services, Newton Mearns might as well have been on the other side of the country as far as Mum and I were concerned.

The three of us being separated was a new experience and difficult to accept, but then living with Dad wasn't easy for Craig either. After a few weeks he found some new friends up in Newton Mearns and ended up sofa-surfing with them for much of the next few months so we often didn't know where or how he was for weeks at a time.

Neither Mum nor I saw much of him, and that was a big thing for me. We had always been a close-knit trio but now, suddenly, it was just me and my mum. Craig had always been the closest thing to a male role model in my life. He was the older brother who looked out for me. He was the reason I was cool in school, but now there were people I had to pass in the street, or share a class with, who hated my brother. He was on a hit list and I was caught in the middle.

On more than one occasion I was stopped on the way home from school by bigger lads who knew who I was and given a 'message' to pass on to Craig. I remember being lifted off my feet and roughly pushed against the wall of a building. I must have been a good actor because, despite being terrified on the inside, my calm outward demeanour was convincing enough to stop them giving me a beating.

At home Mum began to drink more as a form of self-medication for the emotional pain she was suffering. She was grieving for the loss of a child. He may not have died but he was suddenly no longer in her life. There were many late nights, which often slipped into the wee hours of the morning, where I sat cradling her in my arms and helplessly watched as she sobbed and drank herself to sleep with a bottle of vodka. I'd sit there silently, cuddling her while all the time thinking, 'I don't know what to do or how to fix this but I've got school in the morning.'

I was only 14 years old but I felt I had to be the responsible adult and try to pick up the pieces. Once Mum had passed out I would slip off to bed but, as often as not, I'd end up lying awake trying to figure out a way of fixing everything. Frequently I had to get myself up for school and try to function through the day after only one or two hours sleep.

Occasionally Mum would put some of her heartache and thoughts on paper in the form of poetry and prose. It was a way of helping to release the heartache, and although her writings were never intended to be published I believe some were certainly good enough. Even now when I read one of her poems I can relive the fear and sense the anguish. It takes me right back to those days.

Eventually, almost a year to the day after the fight that sparked it all, the case went to the High Court in Glasgow in April 1998. The two lads who instigated the attack, and were accused of carrying out the lion's share of the violence, admitted to a charge of seriously assaulting Gaddie by hitting him with sticks to the danger of his life. They were sent to the High Court in Edinburgh for sentencing.

Although the court was told Gaddie made a good recovery from his injuries, albeit continuing to suffer from dizzy spells for a time afterwards, there is no doubt his life, and the lives of many others including my own, were changed forever that night in April 1997. It certainly has had a profound effect on me in so many ways.

13

Fitba daft

One thing I have learned is that violence very rarely resolves anything. That's why I prefer to keep any drama in my life confined to the stage and find a release for any pent-up frustrations through sport.

Legendary Scottish football player and manager Bill Shankly is reported to have said: 'Some people think football is a matter of life and death. I assure you, it's much more serious than that.' And he's right!

For many youngsters, like me, brought up in the working-class schemes and streets of Glasgow and other Scottish communities, football wasn't, and isn't, just a game. It's a potential passport out of poverty to a life that most people can only ever dream about.

For many generations of Scots who didn't fancy working with their backs down the mines or risking life and limb in the shipyards or other heavy industries – when they still existed in Scotland – there were limited options. They could join the military, run away to sea or try and find something a bit more glamorous, like being a musician in a rock band or a successful football player.

I don't know how many hours I spent as a child daydreaming of playing for a big club, being capped for Scotland and scoring a winning goal for my country, but it was a lot.

Long before any thoughts of acting or entertainment ever entered my head football was, in my young mind at least, the one and only potential escape route to a better life. If I could get good enough to be signed by a big club I could look after my brother and my mum. She wouldn't have to work three or four jobs at a time just to scrape by. We could live in a house with its own front door and a garden.

Many people might dismiss such an ambition as unrealistic, after all, the likelihood of anyone succeeding is very remote. It is estimated that less than 1 per cent of kids who play for amateur clubs or attend football academies will reach any professional level of the game. Out of more than 1.5 million youngsters only about 180 of them have any chance of making it to the UK Premier League.

However, succeeding as a soccer star is still better odds than the 1 in 45 million chance of winning the lottery. Every week around 45 million people in the UK, about 70 per cent of the adult population, play the lotto regularly. They put their faith in luck because they have a dream of being a little better off than they are now or, in some cases, rich beyond their wildest fantasies. At least youngsters who aspire to a better life playing football are betting on their own skills.

Just as someone always wins the lottery, the path to success in football has been well trodden. The rags-to-riches stories of young boys going from kicking a ball in the street to playing at the top of the game have served as an inspiration to millions of youngsters like me over the years.

People like John Wark, who was brought up in relative poverty in the Partick area of Glasgow, sleeping in a drawer and sharing an outside toilet with five other families in a run-down tenement building, are a testament to what can be achieved. Almost as soon as he could kick a ball he was playing in the streets every minute he could, from dawn to dusk, and it paid off. He ended up playing professionally for Ipswich, Middlesborough and Liverpool, along with 29 caps for Scotland. He even got to be a film star, appearing in the 1981 movie *Escape to Victory* alongside Sylvester Stallone, Michael Caine, Bobby Moore and Pele.

Equally, the tale of Denis Law, born the son of a poor fisherman and brought up in a council tenement in Aberdeen, has provided encouragement for many. As a child he had to go barefoot until he was 12 years old and his first pair of football boots were second-hand, given to him as a birthday present when he was a teenager. Despite his lowly beginnings he went on to play for Manchester City, Manchester United and appeared 58 times for Scotland. There are now two statues to him, one in Manchester and one in Aberdeen.

Other players such as Jim Baxter from Fife and George Graham from North Lanarkshire also used their footballing skills to escape the poverty of their childhoods to become an inspiration for me and many others. My one thought back then was that if they could do it so could I.

One of my other boyhood heroes was Steve Archibald, a fellow Ruglonian. In the minds of youngsters like myself Steve could have been any one of us. He was an apprentice mechanic playing for local teams such as Croftfoot United and Fernhill Athletic, similar clubs to the ones I and other boys my age played for, when he was spotted by First Division Clyde.

During his career he played for Aberdeen, Tottenham Hotspur, Blackburn Rovers, Hibernian and Barcelona – who snapped him up for over £1 million – and he was capped 27 times for Scotland.

I, and a lot of the other Rutherglen boys, would often pretend to be Steve when we were having a kick about in the local park.

Football, or soccer as the Americans insist on calling it, has always played a big part in Scottish life, not least because we invented it.

The passing game we know today was developed in Scotland. Ged O'Brien, the former curator of the Scottish Football Museum, has done a lot of great work to prove beyond doubt that Scotland developed modern football and exported it to England, and around the world.

Three Scots – Charles Miller, Archie McLean and Jock Hamilton – introduced football to Brazil in the early 20th century while Glasgow engineer John Harley did the same in Uruguay and teacher Alexander Watson took it to Argentina.

As far back as 1457 Scotland's version of the game is mentioned in official records. King James II tried to have it banned along with golf because he feared the young men were neglecting archery training in favour of playing soccer. Indeed, the oldest surviving football in the world hails from the 16th century and was found in Stirling Castle. Clearly, it is in the blood!

Although I can't remember exactly how old I was when I first kicked a ball and started playing the game I do know that by the age of seven I was addicted.

At home Craig and I took different sides. I supported Rangers and he was a Celtic fan. The small, 10ft x 9ft bedroom we shared was adorned with a mixture of posters, colours and tributes to each team. Blue on one side and green on the other. We would spend hours winding each other up about which team was the best and trading banter.

Over the years I built up a huge collection of Rangers videos and memorabilia. My favourite player was Ally McCoist and I was once fortunate enough to meet him in Greaves Sports shop in Glasgow. It must have been sometime around my birthday in June as I had popped in to buy the new Rangers shirt, and Christmas and birthdays were the only times of the year when I had money for new clothes. To my amazement Ally was in the store launching a new range of boots. The press were there and I was picked out from the crowd to have my picture taken with the great man.

A short time later the photograph was included in the match day programme at Ibrox Park, before one of the fixtures. Although I had never been to see Rangers play, as there was no-one around to take me and we certainly couldn't afford a ticket, one of my mum's friends gave me a copy and it became one of my most treasured possessions for years.

Even though I was never able to attend a match that didn't stop me going down to the stadium to try and get the players' autographs. I really enjoyed meeting and speaking with my heroes, but I also remember standing for hours waiting to see them after training, only for some of the big names to rush past claiming they were too busy to pose for a picture or sign autographs. I remember thinking then that if I was ever in a similar position, I would always make time for my supporters.

Looking back on it now, it makes me wonder just how much of our fate is pre-ordained. Little did I realise then just how important that period of my life was to become in the future when I eventually took to the stage.

Outside the house I was, as they say in Scotland, 'fitba daft'! Every chance I got I was kicking a ball against a wall or playing a game with the other kids. We would use our coats or jumpers to mark out the goals and play matches that went on for hours instead of just 90 minutes. Sometimes there would be only two or three per side while on other occasions there might be 15 or more kids on each team.

By the time I was 12 or 13 I had become pretty good, compared to a lot of the other boys I was playing against, and that's when I joined my first team.

One of my friends knew where Tam Flemming, the manager of one of the local boys' teams, lived. He took me to Tam's house and egged me on to knock on the door and ask to join the club. I remember feeling excited and nervous at the same time. I'd never asked for something that I wanted so badly as this. Neither my brother nor I had ever been part of any organisation as my mum couldn't afford it. We didn't go to cubs, scouts or youth clubs like a lot of the other kids so somehow asking to join Cathkin United football club was a big deal for me. I didn't really believe he would let me join as I'd got used to thinking such things were not meant for people like me.

I didn't really understand at the time but Cathkin United, or Cathkin Boys Club, had been founded by a guy called Jock Barkey who really put his heart and soul into helping young lads like me.

Jock died in 2008 but is still remembered as being a great influence on generations of kids who were given a purpose, structure and organisation in their lives which was often missing at home.

At one point there was about half a dozen Cathkin United teams of different age groups playing at the same time. Jock loved football and was passionate about nurturing talent and the local community.

Talent scouts from other clubs, including the late Jock Stein, would often pop along to watch Cathkin United teams play because they recognised there could be some future talent there.

Tam was one of the coaches and he was really nice. When I suddenly appeared at his door he could have told me to come to the club but instead he invited me in to have a chat. In some ways it was like my first ever audition and to say I was glad to get a part in the club is an understatement. I was over the moon when he said I could come along to the next training night. However, my joy was short-lived. Seconds after feeling elated I was brought down to earth with a major bump. As I was getting ready to leave his home Tam said: 'I'll see you at training, remember to bring your football boots.'

My heart sank like a stone. I didn't have football boots and I knew there was no way my mum could afford to buy any. I couldn't tell Tam the truth, I was ashamed. I just nodded and left. As I walked out onto the street I felt as if a giant rug had been pulled from under me. I genuinely thought my footballing ambitions were over before they had even started and I felt disappointed and angry. I was failing and not because I didn't have any talent or the determination to succeed. My dreams were in danger of disappearing because I was born into a family that could not afford the luxury of a pair of football boots!

The walk home was a blur as I tried to think of ways of raising the cash to buy some boots. By the time I got back to our flat I was already resigned to the fact that it was all over. My mum sensed something was wrong and tried to get me to open up. I was reluctant at first but after some time, and a little cajoling, I explained what had happened and pretended it didn't matter. There was no way I wanted to put even more pressure on my mum so I told her I didn't really want to join the club anyway.

Obviously I wasn't as good at pretending to be cool with it as I thought because the next day my mum came home and said we were going shopping. She had managed to secure an emergency loan – a Provident Cheque. This was something like the payday loans that we have now. My mum was able to borrow just enough money needed to buy a cheap pair of boots and pay it off at a weekly rate plus interest. It was how a lot of families existed in our neighbourhood.

The cheques were only accepted by a few stores so we had to travel a little way to find one that we could use but I was so excited when we went to the shopping arcade. Unfortunately most of the boots they had in stock were out of our price range. The only ones we could afford were too big for me, but I wasn't going to give up. I had thought my chances of going to the club were ruined because we couldn't afford boots but my mum had gone out on a limb to get the cash and I wasn't going home without a purchase.

I pleaded with Mum to buy the boots, despite them being far too big. I was so determined that she eventually gave in and handed over the cash. Even though I had to pack the toes with toilet paper to make them fit I was ecstatic. I had a pair of boots, even if they did make me look a bit like a circus clown, and I was going to be able show up at the training session. I walked all the way home beaming from ear to ear as if I'd already won the World Cup on my own.

Although I wasn't as good as many of the boys who had been at the club for some time it only took me a few weeks of hard work, listening and watching to get up to a standard for Tam to put me in the squad. It might only have been on to the substitute's bench, but it was a step in the right direction to get where I wanted to be – on the pitch.

Initially I was slightly overawed by the organised football training sessions. I was much more reserved than the other boys who all seemed to be more confident, more affluent and certainly more relaxed. It was very strange suddenly having this structure and discipline around me. It was a similar feeling I was to experience when I entered the art world as a newcomer with no background or previous experience.

Over time Tam and his wife Jessie became good friends to me. The boys who played at Cathkin were required to buy a club tie and blazer to wear at games. I suspect Tam and Jessie knew I couldn't afford a blazer, so they 'found' one for me, along with a tie which they taught me how to put on. Even though the blazer was too big for me – the sleeves were much longer than my arms – I felt as if I fitted in with the rest of the boys and was proud to wear it every chance I got.

For a while I played in goals for the team and one night, after I had put up a particularly good performance, I got a lift home with another boy in his dad's big flash car. The boy was in the front passenger seat and I was in the back. I was surprised when the man said I had impressed him with my natural talent and he suggested that I attend an extra coaching course dedicated to goalkeeping. I remember telling him that my mum was struggling for money and that I couldn't afford to do it.

As I got out of the car, just around the corner from my house, the man handed me £40, which was a huge amount of money at the time, especially for me, and said: 'Go to the coaching course, Scott, there's the money for it.'

I couldn't believe it and just stood open-mouthed for a moment until I caught the eye of the boy in the front passenger seat of the car. The look he gave me was chilling and his unspoken message was clear as day: 'Don't you fucking dare take my dad's money!'

I was new to the club and there was no way I was going to do anything which would result in this boy and his friends taking against me. I knew I couldn't accept the cash so I slipped the notes through the window into the back seat of the car as it drove off. It was a horrible decision but probably the right one at the time.

I ended up playing for Cathkin at under-12/13 for the best part of a year or more before being recruited by the older team at the club and ended up playing with the under-16s when I was only 14.

My big break came because some of the lads who were better than me didn't take it seriously. There was one young boy who did really well. He was such a natural talent that he was earmarked for Rangers, but then he stopped trying. He began missing training sessions and didn't bother to show up for a game. When he did eventually put in an appearance he expected to automatically be included in the starting lineup for the next match. He was furious to discover he had been dropped and I was in the squad instead.

The reason I was in and he was out was all down to dedication. The coach told the boy, in no uncertain terms, that although I might not be quite as talented as him I at least turned up to every training session week after week, and I attended all the games – come rain, sun, gale or hail without complaining, even when I didn't get to play and spent all the match on the subs' bench.

Hearing those words made me feel great and I've tried to stick to that way of thinking ever since. So far it has proved to be a recipe for success – the harder I work, the luckier I get!

At least I felt my dream of a career in football was certainly going in the right direction, especially after I was scouted by the coaches from Possil YM AFC, an amateur football club in quite a rough part of Glasgow, but a good team.

Cathkin were up against them one day when I played really well. I was over the moon when the Possil guy asked for my number. It was like being scouted for a bigger team and felt great to be recognised for being good at something. Some kids are lucky, they might not get the positive reinforcement from winning a medal or a trophy but they get it at home from their parents. I didn't. It wasn't because my mum didn't care but because she was never around, working several jobs at a time to put food on the table and keep the lights on. She didn't have time to sit down and give me positive feedback or encouragement for anything.

At the beginning of my time with the club I was able to get a lift to training from one of the older guys but when that came to an end so did my time with Possil. The truth was I couldn't afford the bus fare to get to training. I daren't ask Mum for the money because I knew we were struggling and didn't want to pile on more pressure, so I just stopped going. For a long time she didn't know I had stopped going. While she was at work she thought I was at football but in reality I was staying at home watching telly or hanging about with my mates.

Possil was a great club that had produced a lot of talented youngsters for the bigger clubs. My mum has always said she thought Possil had been a real opportunity and she regretted not being able to do more to support me. It is a lasting regret she has to this day.

After Possil, when I was about 15 or 16, I was asked to join Rutherglen Boys Club. My crowning glory there was winning Player of the Year at the club's annual awards. I remember my mum sitting in the audience at the presentation night and looking proud. I was glad she was there, as she had never been able to come to a match and watch me play. Football had been little more than a babysitter for her. I would go off to training, where she knew I was safe and being looked after, while she went out to work. I'm not sure she ever really appreciated just how big a deal winning that award was to me.

My successes at Rutherglen led to me joining Calderwood Blue Star where I played between the ages of 16 and 17, although I was one of the youngest in the squad.

One of the reasons I kept playing football was that on the pitch I felt equal to the other boys. I was a decent enough player and for 90 minutes a week, and during training, it didn't matter how much money I had, how big my house was or what my parents did for a living. I could hold my head high.

Off the pitch it was a different story. One of the lads I became friends with was called Fraggle. I never knew until much later that his real name was Ryan. All I knew was that we got on really well. We were each about 16, had a similar sense of humour and were both mad about football.

One day, I asked him back to my house for something to eat and to watch a match on the television. His dad picked us up from training and dropped us off round the corner from the two-bedroom tenement flat I shared with Mum. We didn't have any carpets at the time and I remember there wasn't much food in the house so I offered Fraggle a bowl of cereal and we both sat on the end of my bed and watched the television.

The following week I was invited to his place to watch a match – and what a house they had! Compared to our tiny flat, with bare wood floors, empty food cupboards and sparsely little furniture, the home he shared with his parents was a palatial mansion. They had an ice machine as part of their fridge, which was packed with food, and a bin that crushed their rubbish. I had never seen anything like it.

I was in awe of what he had and embarrassed at how little we had by comparison. I felt uneasy and out of my league, even though Fraggle hadn't said or done anything to make me feel uncomfortable. If he had been shocked by the difference in our circumstances he never showed it. He must have been surprised at being invited for dinner, or tea as we called it, and then handed a bowl of cold cereal but he never commented, he just said thanks and ate it sitting next to me on the bed watching telly.

It was only years later, when I understood the old saying 'manners maketh man', that I realised any awkwardness I had felt in developing a friendship with Fraggle was my problem and nobody else's. Politeness, good manners, civility and kindness cost nothing. Those are the qualities which differentiate good people from bad people, not possessions, wealth, rank or title. We should all be prepared to judge and be judged on those traits. Fraggle accepted me for what I was, not what I owned. It didn't matter to him what his family had over mine and I learned to think the same way.

Eventually, my footballing adventure took another turn when I was about 17. The majority of the Calderwood team were older boys so it reached a point when they could no longer play another year at under-18s and they had to go up to the under-21 league.

That seemed like a bit of a stretch for me and Fraggle. Being the youngest we could still play another season at the under-18s level so decided to move to Cart Castle, which later became South Side Star.

We didn't realise at the time just how contentious our decision was. We were valued members of the team and while some of the other Calderwood lads were sad, but understanding, to hear we were moving on others were angry – violently so.

The team was sponsored by one of the local pubs and one evening, after a game, we had all been in the bar for refreshments when an argument broke out between one of the bigger lads, who had a very commanding presence, and one of the other players called Chaz.

The rammy was over Fraggle and I deciding to stay at the under-18s level. Even though we were at the centre of the row Fraggle and I soon left for home. The next day we found out the discussion had resulted in a fight during which the big lad hit Chaz, who was defending me and Fraggle, in the face with a pint glass resulting in a serious life-lasting wound that needed stitches.

Months later the same big lad was involved in another scuffle outside the bar and was slashed on a main artery in his arm. He lost a lot of blood and was lucky to survive. It was a rough place and, needless to say, I never went back to that pub again.

If I had started playing football with proper teams at a younger age my life may have taken a completely different road. However, that doesn't mean that I still don't mourn a little for what might have been.

I eventually gave up playing football in any officially organised way when I got to the under-21s. Up until then it had always been fun, with a lot of banter and laughs. But as we got older some of the boys started drug dealing and there was cocaine being handed out before and after games. One of the problems with alcohol and other drugs is some people can't handle it very well and, apart from the obvious addiction dangers, it changes personalities. Some of the lads started getting more aggressive and really violent on and off the pitch, even with some of their own team members. It took the fun out of it for me.

Although I never reached the dizzy heights of playing premiership football, or representing Scotland on the world stage, I have still enjoyed a football 'career' that has exceeded many of my fantasies.

As an actor, who has appeared in film and on television, I have been fortunate to be invited to play in a number of charity matches alongside some of the greatest names in the game, including football heavyweights such as Graeme Souness, Neil Lennon and my boyhood hero Ally McCoist. Proof, if any was needed, that dreams can indeed come true – just not always in the way we imagined.

14

A blessing in disguise

When I look back on my childhood football experiences I realise how fortunate I was, in more ways than one. Those years were a positive period in my life but, as I get older, I realise that is not the same for everyone.

In recent years there appears to have been an explosion in the number of historic child sex abuse cases going before the courts. Thankfully, we now have a society that encourages victims to speak out and many perpetrators who have preyed on vulnerable youngsters, even if it was decades ago, are finally reaping the consequences of their actions.

In June 2024 I was shocked to discover a coach involved with one of the clubs I played for had been jailed for 12 years after pleading guilty to abusing seven boys in his care between 1986 and 2004. I was not one of his victims but his behaviour towards me had been enough for my mother to try and raise the alarm. Unfortunately she was ignored and he went on to abuse children for years afterwards.

Back in the mid-1990s, when I was aged between 12 and 14, Craig Menzies was a coach at the club I was playing for. He acted as the personal physio for the team which for a young boy like me with dreams of the big league meant he was a figure of unquestionable authority. None of the other wee boys' football teams had a medic that would run on with a magic sponge if a player got hurt, it was just one of their dads. We thought we were much better, more professional because we had a 'proper medic'.

Menzies must have been around 27 years old at the time. He certainly didn't fit the stereotypical image of some dirty old man in a raincoat. He was young, albeit more than twice our age, which meant he was able to say and do things that were laughed off as a joke.

He was the one who would come into the dressing room and rub muscle warming cream on our legs before a match. I remember there was often a lot of messing around. When his hand strayed to the top of a boy's leg the lad might shout

out, 'He's trying to touch my balls' and somebody else would pipe up with, 'Aye, he did the same to me.' Menzies would laugh and say something like, 'Aye right. There's nothing there to touch,' or 'Whit, a tiny wee willie like yours?' It was laughed off and explained away as dressing room banter.

If any of the boys got injured he would take them into a room and massage their injury or put a wee bandage on. There was never anyone else there, it was a one-to-one 'consultation'.

There was a time when Menzies was in hospital. The other coaches told us he had suffered an accident at work, a fall from scaffolding, which had left him seriously injured and unable to walk. We were all encouraged to write letters to him in hospital to cheer him up. I started writing to him, wishing him well and adding that I hoped he would return to the club as soon as he was better.

At first the replies from Menzies were innocent enough but over time they became more suggestive. He would write things like, 'I can't wait to get back to see you sweating your balls off', and 'looking forward to rubbing your legs. Nobody rubs your legs like me.'

I didn't really understand but I must have realised there was something not quite right about it as I stored the letters under my bed. I wasn't actually trying to hide them, I had just never received letters from anyone before and didn't know what else to do with them.

One day my mum was cleaning my room and discovered the letters. There were about a dozen of them. She was shocked at the content and quizzed me for ages about whether anything had happened.

Although I assured her nothing was going on she was worried enough to start checking my underwear when I got home from football for any signs of abuse. She even went to the managers of the club and told them she was concerned and disturbed by the inappropriate content of Menzies' letters. She was brushed off and told that it was only locker room banter. They said Menzies was a top guy and there was nothing to worry about.

I sometimes think that if she had been the wife of a doctor or lawyer instead of just the wee woman who cleaned the shopping arcade she might have been taken more seriously and Menzies could have been stopped there and then, instead of being able to carry on his campaign of abuse for many more years.

On the other hand, our family's relative poverty may have had a positive outcome. I remember being invited by Menzies to go with him, and four other boys, to Newcastle to attend an overnight swimming event. I really wanted to go but my mum didn't have the money to pay for the trip so I wasn't able to attend. I waved Menzies and the others boys off on their trip from outside Rutherglen Town Hall, feeling sad that I was missing out.

Only later did I think our lack of money may have been a blessing in disguise. I don't know if anything untoward happened on that trip but years later, whenever I met some of the boys from the old team, I began to hear stories of how during team trips away Menzies would sit on the stairs of the bed and breakfast, outside the boys' rooms, while the other coaches were in the bar. The boys all had a curfew and had to be in bed by a certain time. Menzies said he was just making sure nobody sneaked out but some of the lads claimed he had popped into the rooms during the night to 'check they were sleeping'.

When Menzies was sentenced at the High Court in Glasgow to 12 years' jail, with a further three years on licence, for abusing seven boys aged between ten and 15, it emerged that one of his tactics was to abuse boys while they slept.

Menzies admitted four charges of indecent assault and four charges of lewd, indecent and libidinous practices, despite claiming he couldn't remember the offences. The court heard he committed the crimes at various locations across Scotland while serving as either a Boys Brigade leader or football coach.

I'd like to think that more than 25 years later behaviour like that shown by Menzies would immediately raise red flags and set alarm bells ringing. Unfortunately child sexual abuse is a bigger problem now than it was then, especially when it comes to the rise in online offences. According to the National Society for the Prevention of Cruelty to Children (NSPCC) a survey of 35 police forces across the UK found the number of child sexual abuse image crimes rose by 79 per cent between 2018 and 2023.

All the experts involved in combating these hideous crimes acknowledge the number of offences remain consistently underreported.

After Menzies was jailed and put on the sex offenders register for an indefinite period, Scotland's Procurator Fiscal for High Court Sexual Offending, Katrina Parkes, said Menzies had used his position to prey on vulnerable young boys and that his depraved offending had affected many who now live with the traumatic consequences of his actions.

She also promised that prosecutors were committed to justice for victims of child sexual abuse, no matter how long ago the offences occurred, and urged victims not to suffer in silence.

I believe we all have a duty to protect children and the most vulnerable from the behaviour of predators like Menzies. If my mum had been listened to back in the mid-1990s perhaps some of the boys that suffered over the following years might have been spared. However, even though my mum's fears were ignored, times have changed. I would encourage anyone in a similar position to speak out. There's an old African proverb that says it takes a village to raise a child. It's true! We are all responsible for providing a safe, healthy environment where children can flourish.

15

Stars in your eyes

Admittedly, school years were not the most productive of my life, nor could they ever be described as the best but they were, by and large, happy.

I may not have been a straight A student, or any kind of valedictorian, but I was capable, dependable, popular and, unfortunately, occasionally obstinate. Indeed, it was that stubbornness, and my obsessiveness over football, which sounded the final bell on my school days at the age of 16 and resulted in my leaving with next to no qualifications for a job in the outside world.

To be fair, my formal education, which started aged five, had been hampered a little by the trauma of being taken away from my mother, albeit for a short time.

Quite a few of my early school reports from Burgh Primary School make mention of my being aggressive and biting other children. It was a bad habit I had picked up in care. I think I had developed it as a self-defence mechanism and I would lash out if I thought anyone was trying to make me do something I didn't want to, or if I thought they were trying to get between me and my mum.

Thankfully, the teachers managed to wean me off the habit and although I still had the occasional playground scrap from time to time most of my energy was diverted to playing football.

It's strange that of all the staff at Burgh Primary the one who sticks out in my memory more than most is the dinner lady. She was quite a fierce woman who would use a big metal spoon to bang the dinner tables to get the attention of all the pupils and then herd us all into the canteen like cattle, making sure nobody misbehaved in the process.

She was a big personality and lots of the kids were afraid of her but I really liked her. I just thought she was putting on a fantastic show right in the middle of the canteen for us all and admired her daily performances.

It was the same when I moved to Stonelaw High School. All the teachers were supportive and I admired a few of them but the members of staff I really liked were the janitors. I loved it when they watched us playing football and would shout encouragement or criticism from the sidelines.

I don't know why I gravitated towards the ancillary staff more than the teachers. Maybe it's because I recognised they came from the same background as me. What I do know is that I learned a lot from them.

Even today, whatever job I'm doing – whether it's starring in a play, managing a theatre or producing an event – I try to get to know the cleaners, the caretakers, the canteen staff and those tasked with what some people consider menial or unskilled jobs. A lot of folk don't bother to look down as they climb the ladder to success. They forget about those a few rungs below and that's a mistake because they are usually the ones who stop the whole thing collapsing. Experience has taught me that if you want some grassroots information, need a little favour done or an extra errand run then these are the people to know in any organisation. If you are nice to them they will usually be nice to you.

Admittedly I was never top of the class, but rather more of a chancer. I remember one occasion of being sent to the library with the rest of my class to pick a book that we could write a book review on. I didn't bother until one morning one of the other lads, who had done his homework, asked if I had done the book review. I hadn't.

I suppose most conscientious students would have panicked then but I thought I'd just wing it. I went straight to the library on the way to class and picked up a Nancy Drew mystery. I had never heard of Nancy Drew. I didn't know what the story was about but knew I had to have a library book in front of me and I just hoped the teacher wouldn't pick on me to talk about it in front of the rest of the class.

I thought I was being very smart and found the wheeze very amusing in my own mind. Unfortunately for me the fates had a different sense of humour and, you guessed it, I was the first student singled out to talk in front of the class.

I should have owned up immediately but instead I decided to try and bluff my way through. I made a big show of digging around in my school bag looking for the book, in a desperate hope that if I stalled long enough the teacher would impatiently move on to another student. No luck, I was forced to hold up the book I hadn't even looked at and explain what it was all about.

The teacher asked: 'Alright, Mr Kyle, what's your book called and what's it about?'

With a completely straight face I stood up and said, as confidently as I could: 'It's called Nancy Drew. It's about a wee boy called Andy whose friends call him a Nancy.'

Before I could say another word the teacher bellowed at me to sit down and gave me a right rollicking in front of the class. I certainly learned a lesson that day but not the one the teacher had intended.

Being a class clown came naturally to me as I had an inbuilt desire to show off and enjoyed making the other students laugh, a trait which was to lead me to taking up acting.

It was at Stonelaw where I got my first real taste of acting. Drama was one of my favourite subjects and although I didn't realise it I was following in the footsteps of some real talent.

Despite being established in 1970 Stonelaw High School is a typical Scottish comprehensive but it has a long a distinguished past. It was a successor to both Stonelaw Public School, which operated between 1886 and 1926 and included the actor and comic genius Stan Laurel among its alumni; and Rutherglen Academy, which lasted from 1926 to 1970.

Among quite a few famous faces to be educated there were pop star Midge Ure, impressionist Janet Brown and comedian Andy Cameron, alongside several premier foot-ballers, esteemed academics, renowned scientists and one-time Scotland's richest man – Jim McColl OBE.

In its incarnation as Stonelaw High School, my Alma Mater can claim to have educated the likes of fashion designer Jonathan Saunders – beloved by celebrities such as Madonna, Kylie Minogue, Sienna Miller and Michelle Obama. It has also produced several high-profile footballers, as well as actors Jayd Johnson and fellow *Outlander* cast member Richard Rankin.

Although Richard was a year older than me we knew of each other at school and even shared many of the same teachers, including one in particular.

Many years after we had left school, and were both working on *Outlander*, Richard and I ended up sharing a car one day with Sophie Skelton and Gary Lewis on the way to a rehearsal.

During the journey Gary, who obviously recognised our accents, asked us where we were from and what school we had gone to. When Richard and I both said we had attended Stonelaw High he gave us both a surprise. It turned out that our English teacher, Charles Stevenson – a man who had played a part in encouraging both of us towards drama – was Gary's real-life brother. It really is a small world!

Mr Stevenson was a really cool teacher. He would let you have a laugh and show off a little but he always knew when and how to get you focused and back on track when he needed to.

Another teacher who I really admired was Mrs Thom. She was fantastic with an ability to command the respect of the class while giving us the freedom to make learning fun.

I remember preparing a talk for the class and asking Mrs Thom how to get a Grade 1, the top mark for such an assignment. I was shocked when she said that in all her

time as a teacher she had only ever once given out a Grade
I to a pupil. She explained the student had used the blackboard and handouts to support the talk and add to the
presentation. Instead of being dispirited by the thought that
a Grade I might be out of my reach I took her comments
as a challenge.

When it came time to make my presentation to the
class I decided to talk about the night I was beaten up by a
gang. I used the blackboard to show where it happened, how
I found myself trapped and left for dead by the side of the
road. I also handed out pictures to the class of the wounds
I received and went into detail about getting part of my ear
sewn back on.

It must have made a change from the usual kind of class
presentations as I was given a standing ovation by the other
students and a Grade I mark from Mrs Thom.

But perhaps the teacher who had the biggest influence on
me and my future was the drama teacher, Mr Roy.

One day we were all in class preparing a new show when
news came through that someone in Mr Roy's family had
died. Understandably he had to leave but, before he went, he
took me to one side and asked if I would lead the class in his
absence and ensure the other students continued working on
the show.

I'll never forget his words when he said: 'Scott, I don't
think you are aware of it but people look up to you and
they want to follow your lead.' Nobody had ever said that
to me before or shown so much faith. He went on to say the
best way I and the rest of the class could support him was to
work hard in his absence so he could take time to look after
his family.

Suddenly the class I had taken because I thought it might
be a bit of a breeze, with lots of goofing around and maybe
a little writing, became very earnest.

I had initially only signed up for drama because there were mostly girls in the class and only three boys. Putting on performances meant we worked together closely everyday and as a result I became very confident when chatting to girls. By the end of my four years at high school I think I had kissed most of the girls in the class.

Drama had given me lots of personal confidence and, like football, I enjoyed the camaraderie of being part of a team with a common purpose. But, once someone I respected put so much faith in me to be a leader I began to take things seriously.

The only time my confidence wavered was when I was asked to take part in the school talent show, cheekily called 'Stars in Your Eyes'. In order to impress some of the girls in the class I agreed to sing and dance as part of a Steps tribute band performing the song 'Tragedy'. There were three girls in the band, myself and another boy, we had been rehearsing for the show most days and, even if I say so myself, we were pretty good.

The auditions for the show were being held in the school hall at lunchtime and all acts who wished to be considered for the final had to audition in front of an audience of fellow students. To my great embarrassment word had got out that I was going to be singing and dancing so all the boys I played in the football team with had arranged to attend in order to jeer and laugh at me.

When I found out what they were planning I bottled it and failed to turn up to the audition. The rest of the group went on without me and got selected for the final. The girls tore me to shreds for chickening out and I felt so bad for letting them down that I agreed to rejoin the group.

On the night of the live show I remember being backstage and shaking with nerves. My mouth was dry and I really wished they hadn't talked me into doing the show. When our name was called I took a deep breath and walked out onto the stage without looking at the audience. At the end of our performance the crowd went wild, even the boys from my football team cheered and whistled, and we were voted overall winners of the show. It was an amazing feeling and something of a turning point for me.

I was no longer embarrassed at wanting to perform and I decided to stay on at school for another two years to do the Higher Drama exam. My performance grades were good and even though I was not as strong on the written aspects of the course Mr Roy was willing to give me extra tuition. It was a good plan and might well have changed my life if I hadn't been so stubborn.

On the last day of term, when a lot of students would often play truant, I decided to go into school because we had a double period of Physical Education on the timetable. For me that meant two hours of football on the new school pitches with our PE teacher, Mr Harry Johnston, who had played professionally for Partick Thistle in his youth.

There was also the added attraction of being able to show off a new football kit and boots that I had been given for my birthday. Even though the rules required everyone to wear the standard PE kit of black shorts and a white T-shirt, things were usually a bit more relaxed on the last day of term.

Unfortunately, although Mr Johnston was okay with my clothing he had to go after an hour and the teacher who replaced him was a stickler for the rules.

I was immediately called out for not wearing the correct uniform and told I could no longer play unless I changed. Despite trying to explain that it was only because it was the last day of school, they were my birthday clothes and most of the other students hadn't even bothered to show up at all, it made no difference.

There was no reasoning with the teacher who ordered me to leave the grounds and return wearing the proper kit. In a flash of anger I declared that I would indeed leave the school – and vowed never to return!

As I walked home and slowly calmed down I realised that due to my stubbornness I had, in a matter of seconds, gone from being a full-time student with a two-year educational course ahead of me to an out-of-work teenager left to survive in the real world. What on earth was I going to do now?

16

A Working Class State of Mind

Looking back on the day I left school I sometimes wonder, with the benefit of 20/20 hindsight, if my explosive argument with the teacher and hot-headed, knee-jerk decision to walk away wasn't some kind of deliberate, subconscious act.

I did enjoy my drama classes and I would have liked to stay at Stonelaw for another two years but I knew, deep down, that as a family we couldn't afford it.

There had been a lot going on at home around this time. Craig, who was now 18 and working as a painter and decorator, had moved out. He was now a young man and had been staying out at weekends and mixing with lads my mother didn't really approve of.

Sometimes he would bring girlfriends and friends back to the house late at night when I was in bed. They would make so much noise I couldn't get any sleep so it caused a lot of arguments between us. When Mum tried to intervene it would turn into a blazing row with all of us shouting and screaming at each other.

As Mum and Craig clashed more and more he decided to move out completely and, apart from the emotional upset that his leaving caused Mum, it left a big hole in the family finances. Craig had been paying £50 a week towards his share of the household bills and suddenly it was gone. While I wasn't earning, the stress and strain of paying the rent, council tax and other bills on her own was seriously impacting my mum's health and wellbeing. Having to find an extra £200 a month is hard for anyone, especially when you're already working every hour possible.

Realistically, I could never have stayed on at school. I had to get out and earn some money if Mum and I were going to be able to survive.

My first thought was to follow Craig into the painting and decorating game so I applied for a college course. I vividly remember passing the entry test and a guy sitting next to me in the exam room asking me the answers. That was new to me as at school I was always the guy asking others for help. Nobody had ever asked me before!

One task on the test paper was to draw a mirror image of half a triangle and the guy at my side asked me to tell him what to do. When we finished the teacher called me out and said that even though I was the youngest candidate sitting the test I had got the top marks of all the people looking to get on the apprenticeship course. At that moment I knew it wasn't for me. If I was getting top marks something wasn't right; I needed more of a challenge. I just hadn't figured out what that was. As Groucho Marx once said: 'I refuse to join any club that would have me as a member. '

After I decided not to become an apprentice painter, I signed on to a government youth scheme that paid 16 and 17 year olds a weekly wage to work with local businesses. Ironically I was given a job in a decorating shop where I worked 40 hours a week for £70. Although it did take some of the financial pressure off of my mum, and it helped keep the government's unemployment statistics down, it was never going to be a long-term career.

At the time we needed every penny we could get because the local authority was arresting Mum's wages to pay council tax arrears and we were left with very little cash to pay for luxuries – such as heating and eating.

There were frequent times when there was no money left at all. We often went without food. When something broke down or was cut off it then it had to stay like that until we could afford to fix the problem. We couldn't just produce money out of thin air and there were times when it was so dispiriting for Mum. She would go out and work long hours, in often mind-numbing menial jobs, only to discover at the end of the month she had nothing to show for it because the council had arrested her wages.

Our financial situation improved slightly when I managed to get a job at the same supermarket my mum had been working at for some time, as one of her many jobs. She put a word in for me and I was employed, first as a trolley-boy, collecting the shopping carts from the car park, and then working my way up to staffing the checkouts and replenishing the shelves.

I was a conscientious worker. I have always believed if a job is worth doing it is worth doing to the best of one's ability. Within a few months, although still a teenager, I was 'promoted' to the fresh food section with responsibility for displaying the products to attract customers, dealing with deliveries and supervising other staff members, many of them more than three times my age.

Ironically when I was first made a 'Best in Fresh Specialist' I didn't even know what a leek was. But, I did know how to display it effectively so that customers were more likely to buy one.

I learned a lot from working in the supermarket and, just like in school, I felt I had someone in the family looking out for me. People were calling me 'Joyce's boy' as they made a point of saying hello. A lot of my mum's friends went out of their way to keep me on the right track.

A job in a supermarket, especially somewhere like Rutherglen, provides an ideal opportunity to people-watch. I found it fascinating to study how customers of all shapes, sizes, colours, creeds and appearances shopped or interacted with staff, friends and complete strangers. I didn't realise it then but I was storing lots of information which I would later use when I had to play different characters on stage and film.

However, even though it was a so-called low-skilled job – albeit a vital one for society as the Covid pandemic proved – it had its challenges and occasional risky moments.

In a poor income area where poverty is a major problem, having to watch out for, and deal with, shoplifters and thieves is part and parcel of a career in retail.

Frequently you would hear a member of staff announce a 'Code 50' over the tannoy system which meant there was a suspected shoplifter operating in the store. A 'Code 100' meant that all staff, not operating the tills or dealing with customers, had to rush to the front door to stop a thief leaving the premises.

My mum used to tell me, over and over again, that if I heard any of the 'code announcements' I should go to the toilet or do something that prevented me getting involved. Rutherglen is a small place where everybody knows each other. She was worried that if I got involved in getting one of the local lads or a junkie arrested for shoplifting I'd end up getting stabbed some night walking home from work, or while out socialising with my friends. She always maintained it wasn't worth getting killed or maimed for the price of a bottle of vodka or a few groceries.

I understood her fears and, in some ways, agreed with her even though I don't and never would condone theft of any kind. But if the store didn't want to go to the expense of hiring trained security guards it did seem a bit much asking ordinary shop staff, many of them middle-aged women like my mum, to put themselves at risk.

Despite her warnings, I did, on one occasion, feel obligated to step in. I know we all have to survive but there have to be lines you do not cross.

One day I was working in the store, restocking the fruit and vegetable shelves when I saw a woman steal a purse from out of a pram being pushed by a young mum. The thief saw me looking and knew immediately I had spotted what she'd done. Brazenly she stared at me, as if warning me not to say anything.

I am ashamed to confess that my first reaction was to look away and carry on putting fruit on the shelves. Then I thought about what it would have been like if somebody had done that to my mum when we were kids. If someone had stolen her purse we would have had nothing, we would have been totally wrecked. I thought if the woman who had just had her purse stolen was in the same situation we had been in so many times then she would be left without any money. It made me angry, my blood began to boil and I saw red.

The thief started to walk down the adjacent aisle and up the next one towards the door. As soon as she reached the exit she started to run and at that moment I dropped everything and took off at high speed in pursuit.

I chased her through the mall, much to the astonishment of other shoppers. She was fast, but years of football training meant I was pretty fit so I managed to catch up with her even though she'd had quite a few yards' head start. As I made a grab for her she fell and we both crashed to the ground in a heap, knocking over a plant pot and various other items of furniture.

People stood and watched with open mouths as the two of us rolled and wrestled about on the shopping mall floor. I was shouting 'give me the purse' and she was screaming back that she didn't have one.

I admit that for one horrible split second I thought I'd grabbed the wrong person and had just assaulted a complete stranger. I almost let go but as we grappled on the ground the purse fell out of her jacket. The police were quick to arrive and she was arrested.

The woman whose purse was stolen hadn't even realised it was gone. The first thing she knew about it all was when two very nice police officers took her into the office at the rear of the store to interview her.

She was shocked to hear what had happened as she hadn't heard all the commotion going on outside the shop.

Although she didn't have a lot of money in the purse, there were pictures of her children and family which had great sentimental value. No doubt the thief would have thrown them away in a nearby trash can if she'd managed to escape.

Grateful that the purse had been returned, she offered me a cash reward but I couldn't take it, even though there was still a few days to go before pay day. It just didn't seem right so I asked that she spend the money on something for her children as a treat. I would have loved that when I was their age.

I was a little worried the police might take a dim view of my chasing after the thief, especially as I had ended up grappling with her on the floor of the mall with her shouting obscenities and claiming I was attacking her because she was innocent and knew nothing about any purse.

I feared they might arrest me and I'd end up getting charged with assault. Luckily the officers said the woman was well known to them and it wasn't the first time she had been in their custody for similar offences. Instead of telling me off they applauded my decision to intervene, especially after I confessed to being hesitant to get involved at first.

After the police had gone I was left to face my mum. I knew she'd be annoyed after all the times she told me not to put myself at risk. But, when I pleaded my case that it could just as easily have been her purse, and the last of our family budget, she understood my reasoning and agreed I did the right thing.

I ended up working at the supermarket for quite a few years. While I was glad to have a job with regular money, the hours could be anti-social, especially when working nights restocking the shelves ready for the store reopening in the morning. As I got older, and became so familiar with the job that I could do most of the tasks on autopilot, I became conscious of needing something more intellectually stimulating.

To quote Colin Burnett, author of the brilliantly funny book *A Working Class State of Mind*, and one of the country's up and coming wave of talent writing in the Scots language: '...there's nuttin maire dangerous in this country than a workin man wae a library caird who isnae afraid tae use it.'

It was while employed on the night shift that I started reading during my break times, and then started taking headphones to work so I could listen to audiobooks non-stop as I carried out my duties. I tried a variety of genres but eventually found myself gravitating towards self-help titles that encouraged me to examine my own abilities, ambitions and self-imposed constraints.

When the uncle of a friend noticed what I was reading he pointed me in the direction of an author called Wayne Dyer – a moment that was to change my life.

After I started listening to Dyer I realised I wasn't a hopeless case. I hadn't failed at anything it was just my circumstances. But, if I didn't like how my life was going it was in my power to try and change it.

Up until this point I was working with, and surrounded by, people who didn't have any ambition or aspirations. They were just surviving. It wasn't their fault, it was how they had been conditioned by the circumstances of their lives.

For the first time in my life I began to think of a future that didn't have to be constrained by my past. One of the lessons I learned was forgiveness. Wayne Dyer's own experiences of how he dealt with the memory of his father walking out really affected me.

Like me, and countless others, Dyer was not born into privilege or security. His own father walked out on the family when he was just a little boy, leaving his 22-year-old mother to bring up three boys all the under the age of four. As a result Dyer spent a lot of the first ten years of his life in and out of foster homes and an orphanage. He grew up carrying an overwhelming feeling of anger and betrayal towards his father. He admitted he would often dream about his old man, of fighting him and then waking up in the mornings sweating with rage.

Those experiences struck a chord with me because I had felt similar emotions and had confused feelings about my own dad.

It was only when Dyer realised that such negativity was harming his own wellbeing that he was able to let go. He did that, in 1974, by trying to trace his father. It was only then he discovered the man who had abandoned him had gone on to marry five other women, had become an alcoholic and died of cirrhosis of the liver in 1964 – ten years before Dyer started looking for him.

After tracking his father's last movements to Biloxi, Mississippi, Dyer went to visit his grave. For three hours he stood in the cemetery venting his anger until something came over him and he forgave his father for everything that had happened. Dyer claimed that from that moment on his own life became better because he was no longer carrying around so much bitterness and anger. Without the negativity dragging him down he gave up drinking, lost weight, improved his fitness and went on to become a best-selling author and public speaker.

His story encouraged me so much I decided to seek out my own dad. I was lucky that my father was still alive and I knew where he was, even though I hadn't seen or spoken to him in years. When I eventually did make contact I was able to hear his side of our story. I had time to rebuild a meaningful relationship with him and his new family, my half-sisters and brother. Rather than being a negative influence from the past, that sat like the proverbial monkey on my back casting a shadow over my happiness, our relationship has grown to be a much more positive part of my life.

The writer Mark Twain once said: 'Forgiveness is the fragrance the violet sheds on the heel that has crushed it.' Both he and Wayne Dyer were right – anger and hatred just lead to misery. The best revenge is happiness and a life lived well. You don't get that carrying around negative baggage.

It was largely Wayne Dyer who set me on the path to try and better myself. His advice of 'don't die with the music still in you' made a mark. I promised myself I would not end up in my 40s or 50s before realising I had been too busy getting on with the day-to-day stuff that all my hopes and dreams had been forgotten or discarded.

I'd never heard anybody speak like him before. Nobody in my world had looked at life the way he did. His analogy of setting up a golf ball on a tee, taking a swing and missing spoke to me because as he said just because you don't hit the ball first time doesn't mean you should give up the game. I was brought up in a culture that seemed to say that if you couldn't do something you were a failure so why try and put yourself through the humiliation. It was like running against the fastest boy in the school in the 100 metres. Why would I want to race against him and come second? My name would go up on the noticeboard showing everyone that I hadn't won, that I'd failed. Through Wayne Dyer I learned to run for myself, to beat my own time and not worry about what anyone else did. It's like business: you can start off with 100 ideas and 99 of them don't work out. It doesn't mean you've failed. You've just learned 99 ways not to do something.

Years later my mate Colin would tease me when I played the audiobooks in the van when we were out on tour with our first plays. He would say, 'Wayne is dire – it's all common sense, Scott, what are you listening to this for?'

I said: 'It's ok for you, you're the son of a police sergeant dad and nurse mum. You are expected to go to college or university, I'm not. My mum said I couldn't go to college because she couldn't afford for me to. I was brought up to think college and university weren't for the likes of me.'

I remember Wayne talking about when he started writing and putting 150 miles on his car driving round trying to sell his books. It inspired me and I took that same approach years later by trudging miles to post leaflets through doors to promote my shows.

All those years listening to Dyer, and other inspirational speakers, for up to ten hours a night, altered something in me. I didn't realise it at the time but I was effectively re-programming my mind and developing a philosophy that would change my life in so many ways.

17

Out of my league

There's a story, often told in some pubs after a few beers among men of middle-age and above, which sums-up the the Glasgow humour of which the city is justifiably famous.

The details may vary but the core of the tale usually remains the same. It revolves around an old man in hospital dying from some unnamed illness while his wife sits adoringly at his bedside, holding his hand.

Weak and feeble, the patient, nearing his final breath, opens his eyes to see his wife of 50 years or more gently weeping with his hand in hers.

With his voice a little more than a whisper, the man says: 'Elsie, my darling wife, you're here!'

She replies: 'Yes, Charlie, I'm here, where else would I be?'

The man stares at his wife and mumbles: 'Do you remember when I crashed my car after losing my job and spent a week in hospital with terrible injuries, and all the time you were by my side?'

'Yes, Charlie, I remember,' sobs his wife.

'And, Elsie, do you remember when I got an electric shock and fell off the roof of the house while fitting the TV aerial? I crashed through the greenhouse and was in a coma for a month. When I woke up you were sitting by my side holding my hand.'

'Yes, Charlie, my love. I remember,' says Elsie, choking back the tears.

'And now, as I near my end from some mystery illness even the doctors can't identify, you are still here by my side, holding my hand,' croaks the old man.

'Yes, darling, that's right. I'm here,' says Elsie with a sweet smile. 'I wouldn't want to be anywhere else.'

With all his remaining strength the man takes his hand from his wife's and looks her in the eyes and says: 'Well, I wish you would push off! I've just realised, you're a bloody jinx!'

I am prompted to recall that story because my relationship with Karen is the total reverse. Far from being any kind of jinx, she has always been, and remains, my lucky charm.

The first time Karen ever saw my face I was just a cheeky wee 13-year-old latch-key kid. I'd like to say, in the words of Ewan MacColl, made famous by Roberta Flack, that she immediately thought the sun rose in my eyes but, to be honest, I don't think she was even aware of me. But, I certainly noticed her!

Karen, who was then just 16 years old, immediately stood out from her friends, at least as far as I was concerned. She was a shy and quiet, blue-eyed, blonde beauty with a dazzling smile and fair complexion who was way out of my league. I remember the day vividly as I couldn't take my eyes off her as she was laughing at the jokes her friends were making. I wouldn't say it was love at first sight, as the age difference at that point in our lives wasn't so much a gap as a yawning chasm, but I knew I liked her.

Luckily for me Karen had recently got back in touch with three of her primary school friends that she hadn't seen for some time. As youngsters they had been pretty inseparable but had drifted apart a little after going to different secondary schools. Her pals knew some of my mates and so our paths began to cross more and more. Karen's friends were attracted to some of the louder lads in my group, who were always messing about. We would frequently see each other when the two groups would meet up at the park to hang out, or gather at each other's homes for impromptu get-togethers.

I got to know Karen a little better over the next couple of years. She was always more reserved than her friends and spent a lot of time in the background not saying much but rather just observing the goings on. Maybe it was her shyness that caught my eye, after all they say opposites attract. I knew I wanted to ask her out but the timing was never right. There was also an added complication that one of Karen's closest friends, Claire, had a crush on me and that meant, as far as Karen was concerned, I was out of bounds. If I had asked for a date Karen would have turned me down in a heartbeat out of loyalty to her pal.

One day Claire dragged Karen down to the parade of shops where I was working in the painting and decorating store with the aim of 'bumping' into me. Apparently they walked up and down the street several times until I eventually emerged at the end of the day.

When I spotted the girls I immediately went into flirt mode and whistled to them from across the road. However, playing 'hard to get', they pretended not to see me and kept walking so I had to run after them. Inevitably we got talking and I invited the girls up to my mum's house at the weekend. I claimed I was hosting a little informal gathering for a few of my more quiet friends. I wanted to stress that none of the usual boisterous gang would be there as I knew it might put them off, especially Karen.

Claire jumped at the chance and Karen, somewhat reluctantly, agreed to tag along, much to my carefully concealed delight. I liked Claire. She was then, and still is now, a really nice person but I always knew that she was never going to be the one for me. Karen was the one who caught my eye but whenever I tried to ask her out she kept saying no and would jokingly, but politely, brush off any of my attempts to get to know her better.

One of Karen's most endearing qualities is loyalty. As long as her friend was attracted to me then any thought of my getting close to Karen, other than as a casual acquaintance, was non-existent. Even though I had readily confessed in confidence to Karen that I was not interested in Claire she still wouldn't let me get close to her until Claire turned her attention to another lad.

And, what was it that finally convinced Karen that I might be good boyfriend material? Was it my good looks, scintillating charm or natural intelligence? Some people may be surprised, albeit not many, that it wasn't any of those but incredibly the way I had dealt with the break-up of a relationship with another girl who had been cheating on me.

I had been seeing a girl called Lynette for several months when my mum's boyfriend at the time, a guy called Gerry, took me, Craig and Mum on our first ever holiday abroad to Tenerife.

Mum had been dating Gerry for a while. He was another big drinker and always seemed to have plenty of cash. He worked as a tic-tac man at the races, communicating the odds between the track-side bookmakers using a semaphore language that had been around from more than 100 years since the 19th century. Once a common sight at the race-track the tic-tac men were a dying breed by the mid-1990s. The advent of smartphones and other modern communication devices put an end to any demand for their talents.

The holiday was big thing for me and I promised Lynette I would bring her back a gift. Gerry gave Craig and me some pocket money for the trip and I remember hanging on to mine until almost the last day so I could get something for Lynette. I didn't have a lot of money but I still spent almost my entire budget on a fake Calvin Klein handbag. It was the best I could afford and I naively thought Lynette would be impressed. She wasn't!

Almost as soon as she received her gift she dumped me for another boy she had been seeing behind my back. I found out later that she took the handbag and destroyed it by smashing it against a lamppost while laughing with her friends about her 'crummy present'.

I was devastated by the break-up and tried to win Lynette back by going round to her house with a bunch of flowers and apologising for anything I might have done to cause the split. It didn't work, at least not with Lynette.

Unbeknownst to me Karen had heard what happened and thought my actions demonstrated a maturity beyond my years which she found lacking in so many of the boys she knew at that time. My forlorn attempts to win back Lynette had earned me a few secret brownie points in Karen's eyes and that's the moment I started to feature on her radar.

Karen had been through a similar thing in reverse when her boyfriend Stephen had cheated on her. The difference was that when she finished the relationship he started a campaign of harassment, phoning her parents, shouting names at her in school.

When she compared Stephen's reaction to the break-up with mine – buying flowers and trying to talk things out – she decided that maybe I was a decent guy.

Honestly, I don't really know what made me behave the way I did after the break-up with Lynette. I think it's because when I saw my mum with the likes of Gerry, Thug, Davey the farmer and any of the other random guys that came and went, I didn't like the way most of them treated her. Every time my mum introduced me to a new boyfriend I would think, 'Right, this is the guy that's going to make my mum happy and look after her.' However, as sure as night follows day, they would either turn out to be a waste of time or they would just disappear. Seeing how those guys behaved made me vow to treat any girlfriend the way I wished somebody had acted towards my mum. I knew from a young age the man I wanted to be was the one I wished had come through the door of our flat when I was a child.

By the time Karen and I finally started dating properly I had left school and got a job at the same Safeway supermarket where my mum worked.

Although I was two years younger than Karen she obviously thought I had something and confided in her mother that she liked me.

When she found out where I worked, Karen's mum, Heather, made a point of seeking me out to have a look at just who this guy was that had caught the eye of her daughter.

To be honest I wasn't that difficult to spot, when Heather walked into Safeway on a mission to track down and assess my character. As a 16-year-old I was probably the youngest person working in the store and, added to that, I wore my hair in what was called a bowl cut back then. It was all the rage at the turn of the century – just saying that makes me feel old – but I was very proud of the hairstyle and it certainly made me distinctive among all the other members of the Safeway staff.

It didn't take long for Heather to pick me out and happily, as I now know years later, I passed the 'first test' without even being aware I was being watched. Heather says she had been immediately struck by my 'work ethic'. I might have been 'only' stacking shelves but, like everything else I do, I was keen to do it as fast and efficiently as I could.

Watching me work hard was enough for Heather to decide to approach me and introduce herself. We had a brief chat and, fortunately, got on so well that when Karen did eventually invite me home to meet her parents Heather was already accepting of our burgeoning relationship. I dread to think what would have happened if she hadn't liked what she had seen during those first few minutes of our meeting in the supermarket.

I didn't know it then but it was a great lesson in life for me. I might have been doing something many people would consider a low-skilled job but, because I did it to the best of my ability, somebody noticed. In my case it was Karen's mum and it helped change my life. First impressions count and if she had taken against me then my life could have been very different.

Karen's family have been, and remain, a hugely positive influence. In many ways their lifestyle was a million miles away from mine. I always remember being outside the arcade in Rutherglen one day when Karen's mum just happened to walk by. I was eating a sandwich at the time and thoughtlessly dropped the wrapper on the ground. Karen's mum immediately told me to pick it up and put it in a bin with the rest of the garbage. I was embarrassed and tried to make light of the situation with some silly comment along the lines of 'not wanting to do a street cleaner out of a job'. It was a smart Alec remark and probably something I'd heard other lads say. Heather was having none of it and I sheepishly picked up the packaging I'd thrown away.

On paper a lot of people might think the relationship Karen and I have would have been doomed from the start. We came from pretty different backgrounds. She had been brought up in a home where both parents were present whereas I had no memory of anything like that; it was a totally alien concept to me. Her family always lived within their means. There wasn't any tick or having to dodge debt collectors. I envied their nice suburban house with a lovely garden that felt safe, loving and secure. They never seemed to have any troubles. When I used to visit there was never much happening, there were no arguments or dramas. Karen's dad would be upstairs playing his keyboard or guitar while her mum was downstairs watching her favourite soaps on television. At first I even thought it was weird that they were in different rooms.

In some ways our relationship was similar to that of my parents, but there were also many differences, the biggest of which was that I was determined to learn from the past and not make the same mistakes they had.

18

Opposites attract

It has often been said that some men are attracted to partners who remind them of their mothers, while women, who enjoy a close bond with their fathers, will look for a mate with similar traits. Although various scientific studies have suggested there may be some element of truth to this, at least for almost 60 per cent of people, it certainly doesn't apply to the relationship enjoyed by Karen and me. We are more likely to fit in with that other well-known saying of 'opposites attract' as the upbringing and early family life we each experienced could not have been more different.

Karen comes from a very stable family. Her parents, Heather and Tommy Cassidy, have been happily married for over 50 years.

Like a lot of Glaswegians of their generation they met at the dancing. Heather was just a 19-year-old bookbinder from Castlemilk and Tommy a 21-year-old carpet weaver from Drumchapel, when they were introduced to each other by mutual friends at the legendary Barrowland Ballroom in Glasgow.

There must be thousands of relationships and marriages in Glasgow that started the same way and in the same place. The famous dancehall, with its distinctive neon sign, believed to be the biggest of its kind in Britain, was opened in 1934 in the east of the city by entrepreneur Maggie McIver, who was affectionately known as the 'Barras Queen'. It has been a beacon of entertainment for the city and beyond ever since.

Born in 1879 as Margaret Russell in the Bridgeton area of Glasgow

Maggie began her professional life running a fruit stall. After meeting her husband, James McIver, in the market, she began hiring out horses and carts to local hawkers who would pedal their goods through the streets of the city. Following a council crackdown on street traders, Maggie started letting the hawkers set up their barrows on her land in Marshall Lane. In a short space of time there were more than 300 stalls operating on the site and in 1926 Maggie built a cover over the market. She wanted to protect the stall holders from having their stock ruined when it rained, a pretty common weather event in Glasgow. However, the move also served to attract more customers to the market, which grew to over 1,000 stalls and the legend of The Barras was born.

Maggie was a very popular character in Glasgow, not least because every Christmas she would host a party for all the traders and their families in a local hall. One year, when the hall wasn't available, Maggie decided to build her own and the original Barrowland Dance Hall was opened on Christmas Eve 1934. Unfortunately the building was destroyed by fire in 1958, the same year Maggie died, but rebuilt by her family as a memorial to her and reopened with great fanfare in 1960.

Over the years the Barrowland, with its sprung dance floor and capacity for almost 2,000 patrons, has become a major concert venue hosting a wealth of big names, including Simple Minds, Amy Winehouse, Stiff Little Fingers, Oasis, Big Country, David Bowie, Robbie Williams and Ed Sheeran among others. It is now a major part of the cultural heritage of not just Glasgow but Scotland as a whole, and is regularly featured in the backdrop of movies and television shows filmed in the city.

Back in the early 1970s when Tommy and Heather were regulars, the Barrowland was just starting to rebuild its popularity in the wake of a spate of murders which terrified the city. The brutal deaths of three young women – Patricia Docker, a 25-year-old, married but estranged mother of one; 32-year-old Jemima McDonald, a single mum of three; and 29-year-old mother of two Helen Puttock – in 1968 and 1969 by a serial killer known as Bible John sent shock waves through the country.

All three victims were known to have enjoyed a night out dancing at the Barrowland before disappearing. In each case their bruised and battered bodies were discovered several hours after they were last seen in the company of a well-dressed young man.

Witnesses at the time claimed they thought they had seen each of the women with a man called John who was heard to quote at length from the Old Testament, giving rise to the media dubbing him Bible John.

There may have been other people who saw the killer but for reasons of their own did not want to come forward and help the police. Back then Thursdays and Saturdays at the Barrowland were reserved for the over-25s, often referred to as 'grab-a-granny' nights, where a minority of married clientele could mingle with the singletons and let their hair down. It was not uncommon to see men, and a good few women, taking off their wedding rings as they stood in the queue to gain entry. For that reason alone there may have been some potential witnesses unwilling to admit where they had been for fear their partners might find out.

It also goes some way to explaining why the teetotal suspect known as Bible John was reported to have been heard referring to the dance hall as a 'den of iniquity' and voicing his warped opinion that any married women who even considered visiting such a place must be 'adulterous by nature'.

The police investigation that followed the murders was one of the largest in Scottish criminal history, involving over 100 police officers who interviewed more than 5,000 potential suspects and took in excess of 50,000 witness statements.

Despite a good artist's impression of a man they wanted to interview – portrayed as between 25 and 30, around 5 ft 10 to 6 ft tall, with light red hair, blue-grey eyes, crooked teeth and a smart modern appearance – nobody was ever arrested. Not surprising really when you consider that description could fit any number of men living in the Glasgow area at that time. Indeed, so many people were caught up in the public's desperation to help police find the killer that the police began handing out printed cards to men they had ruled out of the investigation which bore the words 'I'm not Bible John'.

The climate of fear which grew around the murders resulted in the Barrowland having to live with the stigma of being forever unfairly associated with Scotland's most infamous unidentified serial killer, much in the same way Whitechapel in London remains synonymous with Jack the Ripper.

The legacy of Bible John lives on, over half a century later. He has become Glasgow's bogeyman. His dark deeds still fascinate, enthral and disturb people. The mystery of his identity has only served to create a legend that continues to inspire numerous books, podcasts, movies and newspaper articles. Back in the early 2000s, some 30 years or more after his murderous spree, I was cast to play him in a student production of *The Bible John Killings* while studying at college. The production was filmed at the then Royal Scottish Academy of Music and Drama, now the Royal Conservatoire, where a lot of big names honed their craft.

The project was devised to give film students the chance to learn under the guidance of a professional director who had worked on some big UK television shows like *Only Fools and Horses*. We couldn't film inside the real Barrowland Ballroom so part of the 1960s interior of the dance hall was recreated on a set to record interior scenes of the movie.

As an actor there are different challenges when playing a living being or a fictional personality. For the first you tend to try and convey the spirit, essence or traits peculiar and recognisable to that individual. For a made-up character you have more of a free rein to concoct a fantasy persona.

However, playing a person who is all too real but little is known about, has its own particular obstacles. In the case of Bible John his deeds were undoubtedly monstrous but his appearance was all too ordinary. That's one of the reasons why he has never been caught!

It was only a few days filming but the role has stuck in my mind, not least because it was my first on-screen sex scene, involving the rape and murder of one of the killer's victims. As an adult I'd never kissed anyone other than Karen so having to be so intimate in public with someone I'd only just met was pretty uncomfortable.

Fortunately the woman I was working with was much more relaxed and took charge of the situation. Prior to going on set we talked through the scene, worked out where she was comfortable being touched, and how rough the kissing and manhandling should be. These days there are official 'intimacy coordinators' who help plan out such scenes with the actors and crew but back then we were left to our own devices.

When we did the scene it all worked out fine but I remember still feeling that I was being a little unfaithful to Karen. I can now fully appreciate why the late Patrick McGoohan, star of *The Prisoner* and *Danger Man*, was never intimate on screen with any of his leading ladies. He apparently didn't want to embarrass his children by being seen to kiss anyone other than their mum.

I learned a lot on that project, not least that sometimes what is not said is more dramatic than what is. In one scene I had to chat up one of my intended victims and while we are talking in the bar she had to ask, 'What do you do for work?' I replied with the line 'I take out the rubbish', to which she follows up with, 'Are you a bin man then? and I respond chillingly, 'Something like that.'

On the face of it the exchange between killer and victim is pretty innocuous but for the audience, who are in on the 'joke', the relatively mundane conversation is all the more chilling.

That short delve into the shadows of Glasgow's past made me realise just how strong the fear of Bible John, whose deadly discrimination against dancing 'sinners' still hangs over the city to this day, must have been in 1971 when Karen's parents first met.

However, it wasn't the twisted zealotry of a serial killer that threatened to derail Tommy and Heather's happiness in their early days. It was a more pervasive and institutional religious intolerance that they had to overcome if they wanted to be together.

The problem was that Tommy comes from a Catholic family with nine siblings, one of whom died in infancy before he was born, while Heather was brought up in the Protestant faith.

Although they never saw the religious differences as a barrier, their relatives did, especially Tommy's parents who were never able to fully accept Heather as part of the family. Indeed, when they married on 17 March 1973, St Patrick's Day, Tommy's father refused to attend the wedding.

To me, that sort of situation seems completely mad and sad. But, to be honest, if I had never done the play *Singin' I'm no a Billy he's a Tim* I'm not sure I could ever have had a proper understanding of the situation they found themselves in. I find it incredible that Tommy had to essentially go against his family for love and as a result I have the utmost respect for both of them that they didn't let it spoil their happiness.

Unfortunately sectarian prejudice was rife in Glasgow back then and still is in many sections of the community. Years later, when Tommy was working in a factory he became a union shop steward but was never able to rise any higher. When he asked somebody why he couldn't get promotion he was casually informed that it was because he 'kicked with the wrong foot', meaning he was a Catholic. Today such discrimination could, and should, be challenged in the courts but back then there was little he could do about it.

Similar to my parents, a decade or so later, Tommy and Heather started married life in a small one-room flat with a tiny kitchen and not much else. But, unlike my folks, they were determined to make a go of married life and strived hard together to build a solid foundation for their future.

Although both were working when they got married, Heather cleverly made a point of learning to live on just Tommy's wage, and save her own, from day one. She knew they both wanted a family so they had to get used to having just one salary coming into the home. Heather didn't go back to work until Karen was five years old, a full ten years after first becoming a stay-at-home mum, yet they never wanted for anything or felt they had to make sacrifices.

Fortunately Tommy was always a hard worker and a good provider. When he left school, aged 15, his mum sent him down to the employment exchange, as it was back then, to ask for a job that would teach him a trade. He thought he might get to be a joiner, electrician, plumber or such like. But, much to his surprise, he was sent to a furriers in Bath Street. He started there as an apprentice making fur coats. He worked nine hours a day, six days a week for the next three years to take home less than £3.50 in his weekly pay packet.

As a way of making ends meet Tommy took a second job working alongside a friend called Billy looking after the props and operating the lights at the Alhambra Theatre. Listening to some of his stories now often makes me feel a little envious as I've heard great things about the place. Unfortunately it closed long before I was able to tread its sacred boards.

When it first opened in 1910 the Alhambra was considered one of the most advanced theatres in Britain, renowned for the high-quality and lavish spectacle of its shows. It's no wonder it was to become the venue for the first Royal Variety Performance in Scotland, attended by Queen Elizabeth in 1958.

In 1955 the theatre management introduced a new format which was to become synonymous with the Alhambra and a great Glasgow institution – the *Five Past Eight* show.

The fast-moving song and dance variety show, produced to the same standard as any London West End hit, played host to some of the greatest names in Scottish show business and international stars over the following decade.

Hundreds of thousands of people flocked to see the show, which ran for five months each year. Among the stars to appear on the bill were the likes of Stanley Baxter, Jack Radcliffe, Jimmy Logan, Olga Gwynne, Kenneth McKellar, Cilla Black, The Shadows, Marlene Dietrich and, not forgetting, Jack Milroy and Rikki Fulton. Their comic double act as Francie and Josie became a firm favourite with Glasgow audiences for years.

Tommy recalls working the lights one night when Rikki Fulton was sitting at the piano playing 'Rhapsody in Blue'. Tommy had been doing the show for several weeks and the routine had become almost muscle memory but on this evening he got distracted by something and instead of shining a blue light on Rikki, which was part of the act, he shone a white one. Rikki never said anything but the producer Dickie Hurran tried to get Tommy sacked for that mistake. Luckily he failed. I don't know if Rikki Fulton said anything but Tommy says he was always very friendly, cracking jokes and never complained about anything. He was, according to Tommy, a brilliant man both on and off stage.

Sadly the Alhambra closed in 1969 so Tommy had to find another way to improve his wages and by the time he had met Heather he was working as a weaver with Templeton Carpets.

For more than 150 years the Templeton name was synonymous with Glasgow and quality. James Templeton, a farmer's son born in Campbeltown around 1802 began as a draper's assistant before embarking on an adventure to seek his fortune in Mexico. By the mid-1820s he had made enough money to return to Scotland and open a shawl factory in Paisley.

Within a decade Templeton and another manufacturer, William Quiglay, had pioneered a new manufacturing process to create complex patterned rugs and carpets. Sensing a golden opportunity Templeton started a business creating luxury floor coverings for the rich and famous, including royalty, big fancy hotels and millionaires' mansions.

Although Templeton died in 1885 the business carried on for almost another hundred years, employing more than 3,000 people at its peak, before finally closing its doors in 1981. Tommy was among those made redundant.

The factory closure had been largely brought about by a change in domestic tastes and the advent of cheaper carpets from overseas. Where once Templeton's had created high-quality woven carpets for around £12 a yard, the new fashion was for American shag-pile, nylon carpets and they were only £3 or £4 per yard.

It is never a good time to lose a job but the early 1980s were especially tough. The UK was in severe economic shock. Inflation was above 10 per cent, having fallen from a peak of 27 per cent just before the election of 1979, which saw the Conservative party under Margaret Thatcher sweep to power. Unemployment was rising to a level not seen since the Great Depression of the 1930s and the country was entering the second year of a recession which would last until 1983. There were riots on the streets of London, Liverpool, Leeds, Birmingham and other English towns and cities. For highly skilled workers like Tommy the impact of the recession on the manufacturing industry was life changing.

In addition to any outside pressures Heather was pregnant with Karen at the time and David, their firstborn, had just started school. Unable to get a job using his established skills and experience, Tommy made the brave decision to go back to full-time education as a mature student. His aim was solely to improve his academic qualifications to get an office job of some kind, in keeping with the country's move away from manufacturing to become a service-led economy.

It was a tough few years but with typical determination and resolve Tommy managed to get six O Levels and five Highers towards his goal of a new career in the social work sector. As part of his attempt to gain experience he began volunteering at the local Citizens Advice Bureau.

For anyone who doesn't know, the CAB is a registered charity specialising in advising people with legal, debt, consumer, housing and other problems. It was a role he was born for and he was soon offered a full-time, paid, position – one he would work diligently at to help thousands of other people over the next 30 years or more.

Although it must have been difficult for the five years Tommy was out of paid work, neither he nor Heather let the strain impact their family. If you ask Karen, or her brother David, what their childhood was like both talk of nothing but happy memories.

Despite the five-year age gap, Karen and David have always been close to each other and their parents. They still are. Like us, David lives with his wife and daughter just a few streets away from Tommy and Heather.

Their childhood was a happy one, with regular holidays to Butlins and adventurous days out as a family at weekends. Karen says she cannot remember any time when her parents didn't get on and has no memory of ever witnessing an argument, hearing a raised voice or seeing anything violent. A far cry from my experiences growing up!

When I first started dating Karen and going to her parents' home it all felt so unreal to me, like something from a television show. Credit for Karen's development as a person is all down to her family life. Her parents were by no means wealthy but they were good at managing the money they had, and they worked hard to instil in Karen and her brother an ethos for living within their means, respecting other people and making the best of any situation. All traits which I hope have rubbed off a little on me.

When Karen left school she went to Glasgow College of Commerce to study hairdressing before getting her first job as an assistant in a beauty salon. At the time she was at college I was working at the supermarket and when we met up Karen would regale me with tales about what she was doing on her course, what her fellow students were like and her dreams for the future. It all sounded like a fabulous experience but one I thought was way out of my reach. Not only did I not have any qualifications to get on a course there was also the problem of money, or lack of it, to be precise.

One day Karen came home with a college prospectus highlighting the different classes on offer. One course she thought I might like to try was acting, as she knew how much I had loved drama at school.

l was pretty dismissive of the idea at first, after all I thought just because I did karaoke singing now and again after a few drinks that didn't mean I could perform. Also, I genuinely thought you had to be smart to go to college and I had left school thinking I wasn't intelligent enough for any Higher Education.

Despite my grave reservations Karen did her best to encourage me to apply but it was Tommy who finally convinced me. He was living proof that it is never too late to go back to school and I decided to follow his example and bite the bullet.

As I expected my mum was not at all happy when I went home to break the news. Her first reaction wasn't the unconditional support most people might hope for but rather a wholly negative knee-jerk reaction. 'You can't go to college, I need your dig (rent) money,' was the first, and pretty much only, thing she said.

I knew she was right and felt very guilty at even thinking about trying to better myself but then I had what many might call a lightbulb moment. I decided to ask my supervisor at Safeway if I could move onto the night shift. This would allow me to attend college throughout the day. I could keep my full-time job and be able to pay my mum what she needed for us to live.

Satisfied that I had solved the problem I applied for the course and was duly invited to an interview. It was my very first audition, and very nearly my last.

19

I got you, babe

Signing up for a full-time drama course at the Glasgow College of Nautical Studies, as it was then before changing its name to the City of Glasgow College, was an education in more ways than one.

How I managed to get a place on the Higher National Certificate (HNC) course in Acting and Performance still amazes me. For starters, I didn't really have the academic qualifications to get on the course as I'd left school in a huff before doing any Higher exams and I certainly didn't have any previous performance experience. I hadn't even read a book or written an essay since I was at school five years before. However, with Karen and Tommy's help, I sent off my application in the hope rather than expectation of getting on the first rung of the ladder to change my life.

A few weeks after sending off the initial application I was very pleasantly surprised to be invited for an interview, and that turned out to be my first very valuable lesson – the importance of preparation.

The letter inviting me to audition for the course said I would be asked to perform a monologue from memory. I didn't know what a monologue was and totally misunderstood what was required. I naively thought they would give me a script or something on arrival that I would have to repeat. I guessed it was a test of memory or a demonstration of my ability to learn lines, I didn't know I was supposed to find, rehearse and then perform something I had already prepared.

I must have looked a right numpty standing before the audition panel with a blank look on my face when they asked me what I was going to recite. Fortunately somebody up above was looking out for me and the lecturers took pity. They ended up giving me some improvisation stuff to do. All I remember is running around the stage like some kind of idiot trying to be dramatic in some way. In hindsight it is more than fair to say the audition was a disaster. However, I must have done or said something right as the college decided to take a chance and I managed to blag myself a place on the course.

My first full day at college is burned into my memory but not for the reasons most people would probably expect. Although less than five miles from home, the campus lay on the opposite side of the city and in many ways was light years beyond the world in which I had grown up.

The first thing I noticed as I walked through the main doors of the reception in Cathedral Street was how much younger everybody else looked. At 21 I was pretty much a mature student compared to the others queuing up to register. Most of my fellow freshers had come straight from school whereas I had spent five years in the real world, working for a living stacking shelves in a supermarket.

Despite my worldly experience and relative maturity in some things the brave new world I was entering was an eye-opening experience. I was totally mesmerised by the range of diversity among my fellow students. Growing up within a predominantly white, working-class community centred around a handful of streets in the middle of Rutherglen I had hardly ever seen a brown or black face, certainly not among my circle of friends and acquaintances. Neither had I ever knowingly mixed with anyone who was gay or transgender but here I was suddenly transported into the middle of a wonderful melting-pot of people of all classes, creeds, genders, sexualities and abilities.

At first I wondered what I had let myself in for as I surveyed the colourful characters around me. Like most people I probably rushed to a judgement that would turn out to be totally false.

While standing in the queue to get my student accreditation I remember spotting Umar Ahmed, a good-looking

Asian guy with long hair. I'd seen him drive into the college car park in an old black BMW car as I arrived on my ageing moped. 'What a poseur!' I thought dismissively to myself.

However, first impressions go both ways and, as I was to find out much later, I had caught the eye of Umar. His opinion of me was equally scathing. He thought I looked like a NED, a highly derogatory term in Scotland for someone considered to be a non-educated delinquent or low-class hooligan. Despite our instant suspicion of each other Umar and I became great friends. I was even best man at his wedding.

Alongside Umar there was Brian, who was dressed more flamboyantly feminine than anyone I'd ever seen before. Taylor, as she is now known, was transitioning, but back in 2001, almost a whole generation ago, there just wasn't the acceptance or understanding in wider society that we have today. Taylor is a great character and lovely person but back then I'd never seen the likes before.

Gordon was another character who helped open my eyes to a wider world. On the first day we all had to sit round a table and tell each other about a good and a bad time in our lives. I was surprised when he said his worst time was telling his mum and dad he was gay. Gordon was the first gay guy I had ever met, or at least the first person I knew who was openly gay. I remember being slightly shocked as he was the last guy I thought would be homosexual; he never presented any of the stereotypical signs or behaviours I had been brought up to associate with anyone who was gay.

Until going to college my only references were the stereotypes portrayed on television or film and, by and large, such characters were either portrayed as negative, effete or comical. Compared to now, the 1990s and early 2000s were a lot less enlightened.

It's so easy to forget that back in 2001, a full 13 years before same-sex marriages became legal in Scotland, it took a lot of courage to be openly gay or trans, especially in some areas of Glasgow dominated by a macho culture which by today's standards could be considered toxic. It was only six years previously, in 1995, that Scotland's first ever Pride Scotia parade took place. Despite a chorus of homophobic abuse which greeted the marchers from some quarters, I'm glad to say society has come a long way since. Glasgow is now renowned as having the largest, most vibrant gay scene in Scotland and is considered one of the most gay-friendly cities in Europe.

One of the first tasks we were given as a class was to each write down what we wanted from the course. Most people said things like they wanted to appear on stage, be a film actor or star in a TV soap opera such as *Emmerdale* or *Coronation Street*. For some reason, and I still don't quite understand why, I drew a picture of a penny and said I wanted to see what was on the other side of the coin. I guess I was trying to say I wanted to see how the other half live but didn't have the words to articulate that. It has never been about being famous for me. I just wanted to experience a different, and preferably better, life.

I didn't realise it at first but college was a first step to achieving that dream. There were lots of people on the course from a variety of backgrounds so alien to my own and they all had an enduring influence on me. There were some with Polish, Asian, African and other heritages which I had never before encountered, let alone considered as being of interest or value to my own experiences. They certainly opened my eyes and changed many perceptions I had grown up with.

One night, a little while into the course, Taylor phoned me at home to invite me to her birthday party at the China Buffet King restaurant.

When Karen and I arrived at the venue Taylor had long hair extensions down to the middle of her backside. She was dressed in long black PVC gloves, a fishnet top, black leather trousers and big high heels. She is very tall and the heels made her almost statuesque. She looked great.

The rest of the guests, all close friends of Taylor from outside college, were dressed in a similarly extravagant fashion. They were loud, proud and certainly attracted a lot of attention from the other diners. If anything Karen and I were the ones who looked out of place as we were comparatively underdressed. A few months previously I would undoubtedly have felt very uncomfortable among Taylor and her friends. But now, as we sat down to eat, I was totally relaxed and grateful to be accepted into their company.

However, not everyone was happy. Behind us, on the next table, there was a bunch of lads on a football club night out. As the evening wore on and drinks were consumed I heard a few things, mostly very derogatory comments, coming from the football party. At one point I was walking past their table when one of them said something rude about whether Taylor was a man or a woman. I could sense things could be about to turn ugly. I immediately replied: 'She's a big darlin', isn't she? Come on I'll introduce you.'

Without waiting for a reply I took the arms of the ringleader and guided them all over to meet Taylor. I was able to talk to them about football, as that's my world, and soon the tension began to dissipate. Within a short time both tables had joined together with Taylor and I up on stage singing Sonny and Cher's hit 'I Got You Babe' on the karaoke. By the end of the night everybody was chatting like they were best friends. Taylor especially loved it as the young, handsome football players took turns to get up and dance with her.

That night was not the only moment to have an impact on me. Many of the other students on the course were flamboyantly artistic, certainly compared to me, in the way they dressed, spoke or behaved. There were numerous occasions when I'd feel totally out of place when they were all sitting around talking about their favourite plays, books or films. I was just the wee boy from Rutherglen who played fitba and the force of my 'imposter syndrome' was strong. I didn't know whether to run or stay, it was almost overwhelming. Looking back I'm so glad I decided to hang on in there as apart from being schooled in acting and performance I also learned a lot about humanity. Undoubtedly I fell in love with the people at college more than I did with the acting. I really enjoyed being around folk with creative minds and did my best to soak it all up.

Having entered into a world that was at times both terrifying and exhilarating I thought that if I was going to be an actor I could learn a lot by reading up on body language. More than half of our ability to interact with others comes from the use of non-verbal communication skills.

Sometimes it's not what people say but what they don't that speaks volumes. The twitch of a lip, raising of an eyebrow, blink of an eye or even our posture can convey a range of emotions or intentions. The days of silent movies in which famous actors such as Charlie Chaplin and Buster Keaton had to rely on non-verbal communication to give a great performance may be over but the skills they demonstrated are as important now as they were then, just perhaps a little more subtle.

Among a long list of top performers renowned for being masters of non-verbal acting are Clint Eastwood, Cillian Murphy, Tom Hardy and the late Alan Rickman. Watching them on film is a master class for anyone who wants to learn the strategy of 'less is more'. As John Wayne famously said: 'Talk low, talk slow and don't say too much.'

In my search for knowledge I became a regular at my local library in Rutherglen where I would spend hours scouring the shelves for anything that would inspire me to succeed.

Unlike my fellow students I had to continue working full time in order to afford my tuition and to help with the family finances. I was still living at home and contributing to the household bills so I couldn't just give up my supermarket job and become a full-time student.

I would do four ten-hour night shifts a week, from 10pm to 8am, stacking shelves and then get on my moped each weekday morning and travel to college in my supermarket uniform. Some days my classes didn't start until 12 but I knew that if I went home I might miss my alarm, so I'd go to college, find a corner to sleep in and hope one of my classmates woke me up just before the class was about to start. I did that for three years. It was tough but by the end of the first year I was the only student with a 100 per cent attendance record.

I think I get my work ethic from my mum. It's amazing how a person can get by on just three hours sleep a night. Being able to complete my college course with honours while simultaneously working full time taught me a very valuable lesson. I could so easily have given up and decided it was too difficult but I learned that to achieve anything worthwhile one shouldn't dwell on problems but rather search for solutions.

20

A little charm and a lot of cheek

College was fun but within 18 months I began to look to the future. I knew acting was a tough profession but unless I could make a living from show business then my three years of study were going to have been a complete waste of time and money.

I first realised the odds of becoming a successful working actor were stacked against me when I met a former student from my course in Glasgow. Andrew Stephenson had been a year ahead of me and was regarded as one of the most talented among his peers. There was no doubt in the minds of any of us following in his footsteps that he was going to be somebody and it gave us a huge amount of inspiration.

After leaving college with praise for his student performances ringing in his ears Andy had gone to London, like numerous Scottish actors before him, to make his fame and fortune. Several months later I bumped into him in Glasgow and was eager to ask how well he was doing. At the very least I thought he might have secured a part in a West End show or upcoming television drama.

However my excitement quickly turned to disappointment when he told me that he had been forced to swap the spotlight of the theatre for the neon lights of Pizza Hut. Instead of topping the bill he was topping pizzas. He just couldn't get a break! I was devastated. I thought if an actor as talented as him couldn't get a job in the industry what chance would I have?

A study by researchers at Queen Mary University of London, carried out before the global Covid outbreak, found that only about 2 per cent of performers make a living and more than 90 per cent are out of work at any one time. It wasn't much better back in 2003 when I met Andy.

Years ago a jobbing actor could make a living by joining a resident theatre company, possibly a regional troupe, performing several plays in rotation for one particular venue.

The history of regional repertory theatre can be traced back to 1908 when patron and manager Annie Horseman founded the first such company in Britain at the Gaiety Theatre in Manchester. The idea was such a success that similar companies soon followed in Liverpool, at the Citizens Theatre in Glasgow and across the UK.

Throughout the 20th century, especially the first half, regional repertory theatre provided an invaluable stepping stone for a variety of artists who went on to become major stars, including the likes of Richard Todd, Sir Laurence Olivier, Peter O'Toole, Dame Judi Dench, Sir Ian McKellen, Imelda Staunton, Dirk Bogarde, Brian Cox and Patrick Stewart among many others.

By the time I was embarking on my acting career the golden age of rep was well and truly over. Although there are some companies and theatres keeping the tradition alive the chance of getting a job with one of them was, and still is, increasingly difficult in the face of so much competition. With more than 100 institutions across the UK offering courses and qualifications in some kind of theatre or performance training there are thousands of starry-eyed newcomers entering the business each year to chase a diminishing number of roles and opportunities.

While the college taught me a lot about show it didn't provide much training in business. The emphasis was almost entirely on learning how to perform and much less so on becoming a professional actor or a one-man brand.

When I realised the scale of the challenge, the first thing I did was to ask my lecturers how I could get a job. Their answers were pretty vague. The best advice I got from them was along the lines of I should apply to a theatre like the Citizens and audition for their repertory company. However, the reality was and probably still is, that the chances of somebody like me from the City of Glasgow College getting picked above a candidate from the Royal Conservatoire of Scotland or such like was pretty low. The sad fact is most people who train as actors do not end up as actors, especially those that come from families like mine. Scandalously, in the third decade of the 21st century only 16 per cent of people in the creative industry come from working-class backgrounds.

That's the challenge of any young person trying to get an acting job straight from college. It's not like when you qualify as a doctor and can walk into a hospital and say, 'You're looking for a doctor and I'm a doctor give me a job'. It is very different in acting. You can be the most talented person in the world but you might not get a role or a job because you're too thin, too fat, too small, too tall, your head is the wrong shape. There are loads of reasons.

Faced with this unwelcome, but not so unsurprising, revelation, I was faced with three choices. I could give up entirely and try to forge a career in the supermarket sector; keep trying in the vain hope that fortune would eventually smile on me; or try to make my own luck.

I've never been one for following the path of least resistance or accepting the status quo because 'that's how things have always been done'. Sometimes we achieve success because we don't know it's supposed to be impossible. So, working on the premise that for opportunity to knock you sometimes have to build a door, I chose the last one and decided to set up my own theatre company.

There were plenty of people, much older and more experienced, who thought I was totally insane. But, when I looked around at my fellow students I felt a need to do something. I had become fond of everyone on my course and was convinced we had an amazing pool of talented actors who could sing, dance and turn their hands to almost anything. I thought the shows we had done at college as part of our training were fantastic and they deserved more than just a few performances in front of friends and family. We had all put our hearts and souls into these productions, and the course overall, so it really hurt when I realised that despite our best efforts we were almost all expected to fail.

There is a lot to be said for being young, enthusiastic and blessedly naive. So, aged just 22, and in only the second year of my three-year course, without any experience of the entertainment industry, I set up the No Limit People (NLP) Theatre Company.

At the outset I couldn't see why there should be anything to stop us. Had I realised just how difficult the journey ahead would be I might have had second thoughts but to paraphrase Donald Rumsfeld, the former US Secretary of Defense: 'There are things we know that we know. There are things that we know we don't know. But there are also things we don't know we don't know.'

The first play I decided to produce was *Passing Places* by Stephen Greenhorn, creator of *River City* and the man behind the story of *Sunshine on Leith*, showcasing the songs of The Proclaimers.

Passing Places is a great Scottish comedy as it revolves around two twenty-something guys, Alex and Brian, from Motherwell who are stuck in a rut and going nowhere fast. In an attempt to break away from their mundane lives and dead-end jobs they steal a prize surfboard belonging to Alex's psychopathic boss, Binks, with the intention of selling it in Thurso, the surf capital of Scotland.

With only a stolen, worn-out Lada car for transport, the duo set off on a 300 mile drive to the northernmost town of mainland Scotland where the surf is always up. Unfortunately, Binks is hot on their heels and the play becomes a high-octane, rites-of-passage road-movie for the stage as it follows the characters from the central belt of Scotland, through the Highlands, to the far north coast. It's a soul-searching journey of discovery during which they learn about the fantastic country on their doorstep. Along the way they explore the likes of Mull and the Skye bridge as Brian, a great lover of the library, regales Alex and the audience with interesting facts about the places they go. It's a travelogue, comedy and thought-provoking exercise all rolled into two hours and twenty minutes of good entertainment.

As part of our college course we had staged the play at Glasgow's Citizens Theatre during the Student Festival. One of our drama teachers, Stephen Cafferty, directed the production and I was lucky enough to be cast as Alex. It was a character I could easily identify with as he was so like many of the boys I had grown up alongside. Alex's journey in the play was almost a mirror image of my own. College was my Passing Places. Meeting all these wonderful people I would never before have looked at twice, or associated with in any way, had opened my eyes to a world that was bigger and better than I ever realised existed.

I knew the play well and I was certain it could appeal to a much wider audience if I could only attract folk from the housing schemes – people like the neighbours I grew up beside, everyday men and women who never ordinarily went to the theatre.

We already had the set and the actors so, with Stephen's support, I decide to take a chance. I hired a designer to create some promotional posters and booked East Kilbride Arts Centre as the first stop on our very limited 'world tour'. Having invested my own money I was now 100 per cent committed to producing the show. However, I never realised just what a huge learning experience it was going to be.

One of the first things I discovered is that everybody's quite happy to be centre stage when the spotlight is on them but there is a whole process behind the scenes that needs an army of people to make any production possible. I enjoyed the acting and, luckily, unlike most of the rest of the cast, I was also willing to do the horrible bits nobody else wanted to do. Things like taking care of the door-to-door promotions, overseeing the booking of theatres, finding sponsorship, borrowing transport and securing rehearsal space are all highly necessary but usually thankless tasks.

Using a combination of a little charm and a lot of cheek I managed to blag some free rehearsal space in the back room of the Royale Snooker Hall in Rutherglen. The management were incredibly supportive and even loaned us their old minibus, which was always breaking down at the most inconvenient moments, to move the set around to different venues.

The backroom of the Royale was a great place and ideal for our needs albeit a little spooky at times, especially for anyone left alone in the building. For as long as anyone can remember the premises have been rumoured to be haunted by a middle-aged man dressed in a 1940s-style suit. Over the years a number of staff have reported hearing unearthly footsteps, seeing shadowy figures, witnessing lights switching on or off by themselves and snooker balls rolling across the tables when no-one was playing. One or two people have even claimed to have seen a ghostly reflection of the man in the mirror behind the bar.

Long before the building was used as a snooker hall it housed a tearoom and before that it was a funeral parlour so maybe the idea of a ghost has more to do with the power of suggestion rather than anything paranormal.

When we weren't rehearsing I was still stacking shelves at the supermarket through the night and going to college during the day. Any hours left over were spent walking the streets around East Kilbride posting leaflets through letterboxes on the housing estates in an attempt to attract an audience. It was tough, tiring work but it had its compensations.

One of the highlights of taking the production out of the college and on tour was being able to put *Passing Places* on at my old school, Stonelaw High School. It was a real buzz to be able to go back to a place where I don't think many of the teachers ever had any high hopes of my achieving much in life, and putting on a show.

I wasn't the only one to be glad about going back to Stonelaw. One of my classmates at college, David Lloyd, was another former pupil of the school, although he'd been a couple of years behind me.

David, who played Serge in the play, was born with a pulmonary embolism. His heart was the wrong way round and had a hole in it. By the time he was a teenager he had undergone several operations and had two pacemakers and a defibrillator fitted.

Around the time we were putting on *Passing Places* David's condition had deteriorated and he had to pull out of the full tour due to ill health, but I know performing on stage at his old school was as big a boost for him as it was for me.

When he was just 19 David underwent a full heart transplant after suffering two strokes in the space of a few months. The operation transformed his life and he went on to gain further qualifications in acting before moving to Manchester to pursue his dreams.

David was one of the nicest people I've met and he loved life. He was well aware that a few years earlier he would probably have died in infancy so was determined to make the most of his second chance. He had been given the heart of a young lad killed in a motorcycle accident and, spookily, when he was told the donor's name was Michael he stunned his doctors and family by saying he was already aware of that. He didn't understand how he knew the name, he just did!

Unfortunately his health problems caught up with him and David died, aged just 28, from a heart attack nine years after the transplant. Another young Rutherglen lad taken too soon.

In addition to being able to work with great people like David, putting on *Passing Places* as a touring show taught me quite a few things about myself. It was around this time that I realised I am just as happy producing a show, marketing somebody else's production or hosting a workshop as I am being a performer. I began to look at acting as just one of the things I do. It's great being in front of a camera or on stage but I can get just as much joy helping other people perform and seeing a full house that wouldn't have happened if I hadn't helped to promote it.

Thankfully all the hard work paid off as the college lecturers certainly appreciated my efforts and entrepreneurial spirit. When I graduated I was awarded the Chris Hunter Memorial Cup for Outstanding Achievement and The Star Award for candidate of the year due to my attempts at creating work for others.

When I was presented with the awards Stephen Cafferty said: 'Scott is an example to all young students, his hard work, determination and self-belief combined with his skills developed at college have helped him achieve his goals.'

It was a defining moment for me. Three years previously I had been a working-class kid who didn't even know what a monologue was and now I was being hailed as a star student. It was an exhilarating feeling but it also came with a heavy burden. I had created an expectation for myself that I was going to be one of the 2 per cent. I was determined to find work in this highly competitive industry and I knew that with a little help from my friends, and the legacy of a kindly Scottish entrepreneur once hailed as the richest man in the world, I would do it.

21

For opportunity to knock sometimes you first have to build that door

Graduating from college in 2007 was one of the proudest moments of my life but, once the excitement of being crowned a star pupil and the mutual back-slapping among my peers died away, I was faced with a stark reality. I've never really liked the euphemism 'resting' when applied to non-working actors. In my case, at that particular time in my life, I was unemployed, pure and simple, and with little prospect of landing an acting job anytime soon.

I had enjoyed a brief taste of minimal success – doing what you enjoy and getting paid, however little, is always an achievement in my book – through putting on *Passing Places*. I had also managed to get a little film experience in a low-budget movie called *Pond Life*, written and directed by the very talented Sean Wilkie, but I realised that was never going to be enough. Years of listening to Wayne Dyer and other self-help guides while stacking supermarket shelves had made me realise the old proverb 'all things come to those who wait' isn't strictly true. Perhaps a better motto to live by is 'God helps those who help themselves'. I was all too aware that for opportunity to knock sometimes you first have to build that door.

I recognised that if I was going to make a living as an actor I'd have to create a job for myself and put on a production. The first thing I had to do was to find a play that would appeal to as wide an audience as possible. It had to be one that I could produce with limited experience and, most importantly, put on with next to no budget.

In order to fulfil such a tall order I resolved to heed the words of both a celebrated genius, Albert Einstein, and author JK Rowling, one of the most successful writers of modern times. I decided that like many a poor boy before me it was time to take advantage of the opportunity provided by a great Scot and one of the richest men in history.

It was Einstein who said: 'The only thing that you absolutely have to know, is the location of the library.' His sentiment was echoed years later by Rowling who advised: 'When in doubt go to the library.' If both of these legendary figures of the 20th century could agree on such fundamental advice who was I to ignore it. And so it came to pass that one rather typically grey day in Glasgow I found myself scanning the shelves of Rutherglen Library. This magnificent building is just one of numerous such establishments around the world made possible by the legacy of renowned Fife-born philanthropist Andrew Carnegie.

Carnegie was a fascinating character. His family were originally weavers from the Angus glens who found themselves dispossessed and thrown out of their home as a result of the repercussions following the Jacobite defeat at the Battle of Culloden. Many people who were never directly involved in the conflict suffered because the lairds they paid rent to were unfortunate enough to be on the losing side. The estates of Jacobite sympathisers were confiscated and many communities that had worked on the land, often for generations, were split up and dispersed to the four winds.

The Carnegies were more fortunate than some. They found sanctuary of sorts on the estate of Lady Janet Bruce, mother of the 5th Earl Bruce, at Broomhall near Dunfermline.

Lady Janet was an arch Jacobite. She used to get her coachman to deliver secret messages around Scotland on behalf of the Stuart cause. The Hanoverian troops never arrested him or stopped the coach because the carriage bore her coat of arms so was therefore thought to be above suspicion.

After the 1745 rebellion Lady Bruce was instrumental in helping dispossessed tenants from confiscated Jacobite estates find safe places to live. Through her influence the Carnegies were provided with a roof over their heads and the protection of the Bruce family as their new lairds.

The Carnegies stayed on the Broomhall estate for the best part of 100 years, plying the trade that had supported them for generations. Unfortunately, as a result of an economic crash in the wake of the Napoleonic wars the family got into debt.

A combination of thousands of demobbed soldiers returning home after the Battle of Waterloo in 1815 seeking jobs, coupled with the Lowland Clearances caused by agricultural changes sweeping Scotland and forcing families off the land and into cities for work at the start of the industrial revolution, meant earnings for traditional weavers like the Carnegies were decimated. The family soon got behind on their rent and things came to a head in 1826.

An entry in the estate ledger of the time, which is on display in the impressive private library at Broomhall House, refers to the Carnegies having accumulated arrears over a period of several years. Unable to pay anything towards the debt of £34.10s, equal to around £2,800 today, the family was given notice to quit their home.

Forced off the Bruce estate the Carnegies moved to Dunfermline where they lived until 1848 when William Carnegie emigrated to the United States of America with his wife Margaret and two sons, Andrew and Tom.

Andrew, who had been named after his debt-ridden grandfather, rose from poverty to become a steel magnate and amassed a fortune of more than $309 billion in today's terms, making him one of the richest men the world has ever known.

Although he died in August 1919, Carnegie's legacy continues to this day. He famously said a man should spend the first third of his life acquiring as much education as possible, the second third making money and the last third giving away his fortune to worthwhile causes. He certainly practised what he preached. In the 18 years prior to his death he gave away around $350 million, about $5.5 billion in today's money, of which some 90 per cent went to charities, foundations and universities.

Among his greatest achievements, to my mind at least, was his funding of libraries, credited as one of the most costly philanthropic activities by value in history.

As a boy from a poor, working-class background, Carnegie was lucky to get access to a couple of libraries during his formative years. As a result he cultivated a lifelong love of books. The knowledge they contained enabled him to transform his life.

Between 1883 and 1929 thousands of libraries were built in the USA, UK, Canada, Australia, New Zealand and numerous other countries using funds donated from Carnegie's vast fortune. One of those libraries was built in 1905, using £7,500 from Carnegie, in my hometown of Rutherglen. It certainly changed my life.

Having decided I needed a play to produce I spent hours and days searching the library shelves without luck until, one memorable day, fate intervened and a book fell from the shelves at my feet. I picked it up and it was the play *Singing I'm No A Billy He's A Tim* by Des Dillon. It was about two guys who support rival football clubs, Celtic and Rangers, and are forced to share a police cell on the day their teams meet in an important match. They really don't get along but their petty banter was hilarious. As I read through the play I thought it was fantastic and immediately wondered why it wasn't being performed all over Scotland.

I've never been in prison but I grew up sharing a bedroom, not much larger than a jail cell, with my brother. He is an ardent Celtic fan while I have always been a die-hard Rangers supporter so I understood the rivalry between the two characters in the play all too well. I recognised the arguments, snarky comments, ribbing and downright pettiness that came out of their mouths. I had lived like that for years. This was a play I could do and, more importantly, I knew it would resonate with everyone who had ever championed a sports team, specifically when it relates to Scottish football.

There are parts of Glasgow where the acrimony between Rangers and Celtic goes way beyond simple sporting competition. It is a fact, not always fully appreciated or understood by anyone who has not lived here or experienced it first-hand, that the enmity between the two sides goes back generations. It is steeped in the history and cultural life of the city and beyond.

The two clubs are by far the most dominant in Scottish football and the frequent and hotly anticipated clashes between the Old Firm, about four times a season on average, are reputed to be worth more than £120 million a year to the Scottish economy. But, there is so much more at stake than just mere money or the glamour of cup titles when they meet.

At the root of the rivalry is religious sectarianism, politics and identity. Traditionally, Celtic is a predominantly Catholic team while Rangers is supported mostly by Protestants. Both clubs were formed in the later years of the 19th century.

Celtic was formed in 1887 and the club played its first match in 1888. It was a way of raising funds for Irish Catholic communities in Glasgow. Their numbers soared at the end of the 19th century with the arrival of countless immigrants fleeing the potato famine of the mid-1800s which claimed the lives of around one million people and forced a similar number to leave Ireland for good.

As Catholics in a fiercely Protestant Scotland, football was a way for poor immigrants to escape the harsh realties of everyday life and express their own identity. Ever since those days Celtic has been associated with Irish or Scottish identity, with republican tendencies, rather than support for the monarchist United Kingdom.

Although Rangers started life some 16 years before Celtic, in 1872, it didn't really become associated with British nationalism or exhibit any real anti-Catholic bias until around 1888 when John Ure-Primrose became patron and chairman.

As somebody with strong anti-Irish and anti-Catholic views he set about establishing the club as a direct opponent to everything Celtic stood for, and that included a policy of not recruiting any Catholic players regardless of ability. For almost 100 years this unwritten rule remained in place until 1989 when Rangers' manager Graeme Souness signed Maurice Johnston, a Catholic and ex-Celtic player.

Even today, almost 30 years later, rivalry between supporters of the two clubs is often cited as the most heated in the world. Aggressive behaviour between competing fans is commonplace with numerous deaths, thousands of injuries and a multitude of arrests, directly linked to incidents involving opposing factions over the years. Various studies have claimed that on the days of Old Firm matches emergency calls to police with reports of domestic violence assaults in and around Glasgow rocket, sometimes by as much as 138 per cent.

As soon as I began to read the play I knew in my gut that it could be a major hit. At first glance the play appears to be a comic characterisation of two bigoted football fans from opposing sides forced to share a jail cell on the day of an Old Firm clash, under the watchful eye of Harry the custody officer.

Billy, an ardent Rangers supporter and Tim, a Celtic fan, are forced to confront their differences and acknowledge their similarities as the play uses comedy and pathos to explore the culture, identity, history and shared humanity of the two young men. Far from being a perpetuation of what has come to be known as 'Scotland's shame' the play shines a spotlight on the absurdity of sectarianism.

I immediately checked the book out of the library and went home to make a plan. To say I was excited at the prospect of producing it as a stage show would be an understatement but I never imagined just how much of a life-changing event this was going to be.

Almost as soon as I got in the door, and even before I took my jacket off, I telephoned a couple guys who had been on my college course. Colin Little and James Miller had become good friends and I knew they would be right for the parts. I immediately invited them round to my place so we could read the play together. Fortunately, they liked it as much as I did. My enthusiasm must have been infectious because they quickly agreed to help even though I couldn't afford to pay them anything.

Once I had my cast I recruited my college lecturer, Stephen Cafferty, to direct as I began blagging some props for our new production. To say the set was basic would be putting it mildly. I managed to talk a local joiner into knocking up a backdrop representing the inside of a jail cell and bought an old second-hand toilet pan from the Barras market.

I also managed to secure some rehearsal premises in the backroom of a local Rutherglen bar for free, in exchange for putting on a show for the regulars once we were ready to lift the curtain. Our first memorable performance was in front of around 60 people in the pub and, to my great relief, it went down a storm.

The next stop was the Citizens Theatre where I convinced the management to let us perform *Billy & Tim* for a week on one of the smaller stages. Again, it was a huge success.

Once I was confident we had a show people would enjoy I began making plans to take it on the road. A good friend, Paul Haggerty, generously gave us use of a mobile phone and an old van he had used for his heating and plumbing business to transport the set and cast around various pubs and venues that agreed to let us put on the play. In the end we took *Billy & Tim* to more than 20 venues across Scotland, playing to packed houses at almost every performance from Jedburgh to John o' Groats.

Right from the start I knew *Billy & Tim* would appeal to more than just the usual theatre audiences. Everywhere we went was preceded by weeks of promotions. Karen, myself, my friends and family members spent hours, days and weeks tramping around the numerous housing estates of Glasgow posting flyers through letter boxes, putting up posters in shop windows and pasting banners on lamp posts advertising the show. The result was that we attracted football fans and people who had never before attended a live theatre performance. It was a story ordinary folk could identify with and became such a crowd-puller that the papers described *Billy & Tim* as 'Scottish theatre's greatest success story of recent times' grossing over £1 million at the box office over five years.

In 2010 we took the show to the Edinburgh Fringe where we continued to hone our more unusual marketing techniques. Unhappy at the lack of promotion being given to the show by the Edinburgh venue we were playing I fell out with the box office manager when he told me bluntly that he didn't like the way we were publicising the show.

I guess in many ways we were very loud and did a lot of an 'in your face' style of marketing. We would go out into the streets of Edinburgh and act as though we were hawking stuff at the Barras market in Glasgow, drumming up audiences like we were selling sports socks or knock-off towels.

There are lot of companies that go to the Fringe with the bank of mum and dad or access to other funds behind them. They don't need to worry about pulling in audiences as it is just a bit of a holiday for them during a break from university. They can afford to swan around, attending cheese and wine parties while trying to network and make contacts for an aspiring career in television or whatever. Unfortunately, neither I nor the rest of the cast had that luxury. We had to hustle to sell the tickets or take a financial hit we couldn't afford. If that meant being out walking the streets everyday cajoling, charming and encouraging people to buy a ticket that's what I was going to do. Putting on a show means there are often a lot of things outwith your control but selling tickets isn't one of them. That was something I could do to make a difference.

Out of frustration that the venue didn't seem to want to spend any money on helping plug the show I tried to book a billboard close to the theatre. Unfortunately, I was too late as another production had beaten me to it. Undeterred I plastered the side of our van with a poster for *Billy & Tim* and parked it on a double yellow line where people couldn't fail to miss it. I had worked out that a parking ticket cost £30 if you paid it within 15 days, or else it doubled to £60. At a cost of £30 a day it was cheaper to park the van illegally where more people would see it than hire an advertising billboard.

It all paid off when we made a wee profit, which is unusual for a lot of shows put on during the Edinburgh Festivals. To my surprise I was even named 'The Stage Best Actor' and awarded the coveted 'Stage Award for Acting Excellence' for my performance as Billy at The Fringe.

After winning the award at Edinburgh I was approached by some serious producers from London theatres who wanted me to take the show there. I knew I couldn't afford to do it without guaranteed ticket sales and I couldn't leaflet London like I had towns and cities in Scotland.

Initially the producers were willing to bankroll the production but the deal fell apart when I told them that Des Dillon was on 15 per cent of ticket sales. They said that was more than they paid writers like Harold Pinter so refused to take the show unless I could secure a better arrangement with the author. Unfortunately, Des refused to back down. I even went to the producers and asked if they could pay him 7 per cent, the same as they paid Harold Pinter, and I would give him the other 8 per cent out of my cut. They said absolutely not because they didn't want to set a precedent for other writers.

I've always regretted not being able to take the show to London. Playing the West End would have been a dream come true but with the 'gentleman's agreement' I had with Des at the time there was no way it was going to happen. I was forced to keep touring the rest of the country.

Failure was not an option and it never entered my mind. I knew I had to pack out every theatre we played because if, for any reason the show didn't sell out, the theatres wouldn't book us for a return visit the next year. They would want us to take a rest for a year or two before booking it back in. I couldn't risk that because I didn't have an alternative show to replace *Billy & Tim*. I had to ensure every performance was full at every theatre, even if that meant spending thousands of pounds and hundreds of hours promoting the show to new, untapped audiences.

I don't think Des or anyone else realised just how much work and money was going into promoting *Billy & Tim* behind the scenes. When he took back control of the show audience numbers fell off. It wasn't because the show wasn't as good but because he wasn't going out and physically putting leaflets through every door in every housing estate and scheme in each town the show played.

When we started in 2008 we were complete nobodies. When I tried to get my local venue, Rutherglen Town Hall, to take the show they turned it down because it was deemed to be 'too controversial'. But we kept trying, much to the amusement of many theatre staff who would laugh when we turned up at venues in a clapped-out tradesman's van with nothing but a collapsable jail set and second-hand toilet as a prop. Once we made it a success theatres were calling us and begging for the show.

It took a lot of shoe leather and a few years but by the time we finished, *Billy & Tim* was performing to sold-out venues across Scotland, and Ireland, including before a 3,000-capacity audience at the Scottish Exhibition Centre in Glasgow.

We were feted as a cultural phenomenon as the show brought people together from across the Catholic–Protestant divide and united them in laughter.

We were publicly praised by politicians from all sides of the Scottish parliament for helping to fight against the scourge of sectarianism. We took versions of the play into prisons, schools, youth groups, community centres and pubs to encourage dialogue and break down barriers.

For the first time in my life I had more money in the bank than I'd ever dreamed of. *Billy & Tim* was on a roll, taking up to £50,000 a night at the box office and all without any funding or outside financial support. I thought I had cracked it and that it would never end.

22

No good deed goes unpunished

After years of hard work I had a hit show, thousands of pounds to my name and a beautiful girlfriend. But, instead of paving the way for a future of stress-free bliss, that life-changing pile of money in the bank, and specifically my decisions on how to spend it, almost wrecked the most important relationship of my life.

Flush with cash and the invincibility of youth I thought the golden goose that was *Billy & Tim* would go on forever. I didn't stop to think the money I'd saved so far would run out. As far as I was concerned the show I had taken from nothing to earning mind-blowing riches at the box office would run and run and run.

So, it was with a great sense of smug pride that I walked into the council offices in Rutherglen one day and paid off my mother's council tax arrears, amounting to almost £6,000, in a single payment. To some people that sum might seem quite trivial, after all compared to the price of a new car or property it is a drop in the ocean. But, to somebody like me, from my background, who as a boy used to wait outside the chip shop at the close of business in the hope of getting free scraps, just having such an amount of money at my disposal all in one go was a fantasy come true.

For anyone unfamiliar with the concept, council tax is an annual fee almost everyone pays to their local authority. It is a tax set by the council and used to fund local services such as street cleaning, community centres, libraries and such like.

Not paying the council tax is an offence. Local authorities need the money to fund vital services but yet each year there are many thousands of families who simply can't afford to pay. For years we had been like that. When my mum had to choose between putting food on the table or paying the tax then it was the council that had to wait for their money.

Where I was brought up hardly anybody paid the council tax on time, if at all. Lots of people were always behind in their payments, just like us. However, I recall vividly the anxiety that came each morning when the postman arrived over the fear of getting letters from the council threatening us with court action if we didn't pay. There was always a danger the council would get a court warrant to arrest my mum's wages, which they did a number of times. The authorities had no idea what it had been like for us and what a massive impact it had in our house. There were times we went without food or the power and heating would get cut off.

Usually, like most people, we would have to negotiate with a debt collecting agency to pay the arrears off at a lesser amount each month to avoid further court action. This meant my mother was never free of debt as the payments would drag on for years and years, only interrupted occasionally when she defaulted on the arrangement and the whole circle of court judgements, debt collectors and new arrangements would start again.

I remember some nights feeling so inadequate. I was 14, my brother had gone, my mum was an emotional wreck, there was nothing to eat, we had no money and I didn't have any skills to get some. I was just a schoolboy yet I was already being made to feel like I'd failed somehow and that I was useless.

The day I walked into the council offices to pay my mum's arrears was therefore a very big moment for me, or at least I thought so at the time. I remember the lassie behind the counter was completely gobsmacked. She had never seen anybody do something like this before. She even had to get her supervisor to come and deal with me as it was such a large amount of money in one go. Indeed, it was so unusual other people came out from the back office to see what was happening.

When I explained what I was trying to do both the lassie and her boss were full of praise about what a good thing

I was doing, how lucky my mum was, how proud and grateful she must be, and what a great son I was. I admit I enjoyed the praise. It was, I imagined, like getting a standing ovation, a prestigious film award and the starring role in my own blockbuster movie all at the same time.

The feeling was great so I decided to go further. I had already paid off the remainder of my mum's mortgage, which had about ten years left to run, and had her flat completely redecorated one weekend when she was away. High on the thought I was doing something good, I also settled all of my mother's outstanding credit card debts. In total I probably spent more than £30,000.

But, as the saying goes, 'pride comes before a fall'. My sudden nosedive to reality wasn't the result of a gentle tumble but more like a headlong push from a tall building. I thought my mum would be proud and happy, maybe even tearfully ecstatic, but when I told her about the council tax she was furious!

There were lots of other things she would have rather done with the cash than pay the council. As far as she was concerned I'd wasted the money. All I had done was to stop her getting a few nasty letters and not made her life any better.

I felt crushed. And it didn't stop there.

Around this time I had been living on and off with Karen in a flat she'd bought with her life savings and money borrowed from her parents. I was still paying rent to my mum but Karen and I had talked about me buying half of the flat from her, paying back her parents, and then us getting a joint place together so we could set up home properly. However, I couldn't just walk out on my mum as she needed my rent money. I thought if I paid off all my mum's debts I would make more money to buy a place with Karen and we could then start a family in a few years, maybe.

I remember clearly the night I told Karen I'd spent most of my savings from *Billy & Tim* on my mum. We were in the Blue Dog pub when I confessed all and it certainly didn't go as I'd imagined.

Although I was pretty much living with Karen I had still been paying a number of my mum's bills, so Karen had been paying the lion's share of the costs of the home we shared. Up until that point I don't think Karen really knew how much I was still supporting my mum financially and to my shame I never really thought to tell her.

To this day I still don't know exactly what I was expecting Karen to say but I certainly wasn't ready for the reaction I got. Maybe I thought she'd be like the women in the council offices and say what a good son I was. Instead she just froze, hesitated for what seemed like an age and said: 'What did you do that for?'

At that time Karen was 28 and I was 26. I knew she was ready to get married, buy a home for us and desperately wanted to start a family but those things cost money. Karen's upbringing was such that she wasn't going to do any of that until she could afford it. But, the chances of us having enough money while I was still supporting my mother to the tune of tens of thousands of pounds meant Karen was unlikely to realise any of her dreams soon, at least with me. That £30,000 could have gone a long way to building a life for us.

It was one of the few times Karen has ever shown any real anger towards anything I have done. In my haste to do something nice I neglected the key component in any good relationship, communication.

Karen was devastated, especially as she had played such a major part in helping me to get the money in the first place. She had been beside me every day and night as we trudged for miles around the streets of Glasgow pushing flyers through doors to promote the show. In the rain, sun, sleet and snow she had been the one constant by my side helping to promote *Billy & Tim* to people who would otherwise never have thought of going to the theatre. She had worked hard to help make the show the success it was and I'd gone and blown almost everything we had earned.

For years she had been working her arse off trying to build a life with me and didn't quite understand the relationship I had with my mum. For too long after Craig left it had just been Mum and me. I had been the 'man of the house'. I'm the one who put her to bed when she was drunk. I paid £50 a week towards the rent and bills when I was only earning about £120 a week.

Karen's family couldn't have been more different to mine. They were savers. I never had any savings and as much as I might have wanted to move out of my mum's home I couldn't because she needed the money I paid her for my board to keep a roof over her head.

Karen's folks didn't drink, smoke or go out every week socialising. As a result they have been able to have a comfortable life with three holidays a year, a nice house and savings in the bank. In our house my mum juggled multiple minimum wage jobs. She also smoked, drank and socialised so there was never any spare cash.

Karen is very much like her parents, very hands-on. She is the one always willing to try a bit of DIY, decorating or repairing things that go wrong. I was brought up in a house where I was constantly told not to touch anything that broke until a man came to sort it. Considering how many times we were short of money there were a lot of things in our house that never got fixed because we couldn't afford to pay somebody for the repairs.

When you think of our different backgrounds Karen and I have a romance which is very much a lady and the tramp type of scenario. Her parents have been together for years in a very settled and loving relationship. They have a happy family with no drama, drunkenness or violence and live in a better end of Rutherglen. Karen is well spoken and well brought up while I'm just the boy from the scheme.

All too often kids who don't have a structure at home, parents who can't help with homework or show them the attention they need go off the rails because the schools think they don't want to take lessons seriously. Some youngsters might be like that but others do want to learn but maybe don't know how. They then live up to the expectations they think others have of them. That's when they become the class clown or a school dropout.

I was lucky meeting Karen and her parents. I saw in her father, Tommy, a man who went back to education and changed his life. I saw Heather as a woman who supported her family and helped bring structure to their lives. It changed me as it inspired me to go back to college and study drama.

Even when I couldn't see it Karen recognised that my mum was sometimes too reliant on me, and I was probably too quick to give her anything she wanted if I could. My mum just had to drop a hint about wanting a new sofa or some other things she liked and I would get out my credit card and buy it for her.

I had always felt responsible for my mum. There were times when she was bubbly and happy and then suddenly she would go dark and get deeply depressed about her money worries. That would often result in her smoking and drinking more, and being vulnerable to getting involved in disastrous, toxic relationships. I thought it was part of my journey, my job in a way, to try and fix my mum before I could start to make a life for myself and Karen.

For her part Karen was starting to think I was choosing my mum over her. She thought my not telling her about spending all that money on my mum was somehow a betrayal or deception. Honesty had always been our thing. Mutual trust and respect played a big part in our relationship. My actions endangered that bond because Karen felt let down. As far as I know that is the only time, in all the years we have been together, where she has had doubts about our relationship and whether it was worth continuing. To this day I am eternally grateful she decided to stick by me.

23

You never truly appreciate what you have until it's gone

They say you never truly appreciate what you have until it's gone or, as in my relationship with Karen, you come close to losing it.

For years I had known Karen was ready to settle down and start a family while I was much more hesitant. It's often a cliche that men are afraid of commitment but in some ways I was. While Karen saw marriage and family as a logical progressive step in our relationship the thought of making it official was frightening, even though I was absolutely certain there was never going to be anyone else for me.

I believe the difference in our expectations and dreams lies in our family backgrounds. Her parents had always been together. They were in a stable, loving relationship and the example they had set for Karen and her brother projected a positive image of marriage.

On the other hand I came from a broken home where there was always something kicking off, an atmosphere of fear or sense of foreboding. My mum and dad had stood in front of an altar and promised to love, honour and cherish one another and almost the exact opposite had happened. They made the same promises Tommy and Heather did but my parents couldn't keep them. I saw it happen again and again to so many people in the community where I grew up. I knew of guys, and girls, who would get engaged even though they were messing around with other people before they even walked down the aisle. They would get married in a fanfare of frivolity, have children, split up – usually acrimoniously – and get divorced. Their kids would end up like me and I was determined any child of mine would not have to go through the kind of upbringing I experienced.

In the same way Bjorn Borg never shaved before Wimbledon, Serena Williams ties her shoelaces a specific way and Cristiano Ronaldo has to be the last out of the tunnel before a match I didn't want to risk jinxing what I had with

Karen. I thought the longer we were together without getting engaged or married the more real it was and more likely it was to last.

I always thought Karen was out of my league, especially when I first met her. More popular and much better-looking guys than me would ask her out and she always said no. I thought I had no chance. Later she admitted that she might not have dated me if I'd already been an actor when we met, and I can understand why. I saw what strain it had on my parents' relationship when my dad used to be away every weekend playing pub gigs with his band. My mum was left behind on her own without a partner. I was afraid the same thing would happen to us and that history was doomed to repeat itself.

The prospect of almost losing Karen was something of a wake-up call. I realised I had been putting off taking our relationship to the next level out of fear rather than for the numerous reasons I had told myself over the years, such as 'once I've made enough money', 'as soon as I'm sure my mum is ok' or 'after I have established a clear career path'. I had procrastinated long enough!

Deciding to propose to Karen wasn't difficult but working out when and how were a little more problematic. After 13 years together I was pretty sure she would say yes but I wanted it to be special, memorable and as romantic as possible. If nothing else, I believed she deserved at least that much for having waited so long and put up with me all this time.

My mind made up, I'd been carrying the ring around for weeks waiting for the most romantic moment, like something from a movie. But there never seemed to be the right moment, when everything felt just right.

I thought of whisking her away somewhere romantic but I was working all the time. I then had the idea of making a grand gesture by asking her on stage in front of 3,000 people at the SECC after a performance of *Billy & Tim*, but I chickened out at the last minute.

Instead, all my ideas of a romcom-style climax in an idyllic setting came to nothing and my proposal turned out to be much more ordinary than anything I could have planned for, and probably more heartfelt because of it.

One night, we were sitting in Karen's flat watching a soap show on television. It's not something I usually enjoy so I can't even remember which one. I was watching the show because Karen enjoys them and suddenly I thought this was what marriage was all about; spending time together even when it means doing something you don't really want to do because it makes your other half happy and you're happy that they are happy.

I was a big fan of the song 'Marry Me' by Train and I used to listen to it in the van with the guys when we were on tour. The other blokes used to laugh at me liking that song because they knew I'd been with Karen for years without being engaged.

When the TV soap finished I said I had a new CD and put it on for us to listen to. I went down on one knee to put the CD into the player and Karen was lying next to me. As soon as the song 'Marry Me' came on I turned and opened the box containing the ring and presented it to her.

Even I didn't know I was going to propose at that moment so I was probably as surprised as she was. She burst out crying and said, 'Yes! Yes! Yes!'

A few years later we went to Las Vegas where we saw Train and they were launching their wine at the Mandalay Bay Beach. We got to meet the group and tell them about our story of how I proposed to their song – a story they must have heard a thousand times. They listened politely and it was magical moment for us, even though I'm sure they probably get tired of people telling them the same thing everywhere they go.

Once we were engaged there was no point in hanging around for another 13 years so we started planning a wedding. Neither of us wanted a big event so we decided to combine it with a two-week holiday in the sun.

On 28 April 2013 Karen and I got married on the beautiful island of Cyprus. The wedding was magical and one of the best experiences of my life as we were on holiday with 16 of our closest friends and family.

The wedding was a very relaxed affair, even to the point that I was away playing five-a-side football at 11am on the day of the wedding. I remember wearing a long-sleeved football shirt when it was roasting at peak season on Cyprus. One of the other players asked if I was too hot and I replied, 'Yes, but I'm getting married and trying to lose a bit of weight before the wedding.' He then asked, 'When's the wedding?' and his mouth dropped open when I replied, 'In about an hour.'

Being a Scottish wedding a few of us were wearing kilts, an unusual sight in Cyprus. It meant we got almost as much attention from the resort staff and other guests as Karen did in her bridal gown. And, that is saying something! Karen looked absolutely stunning in her white, strapless wedding dress. A clear example, if there was ever a need for another one, that I have always thought I have been 'punching above my weight' from the day we met.

Far from our wedding being the highlight of our relationship, as it is so sadly for many couples, it was the start of something even better and stronger than I could ever have imagined.

I believe the secret to a long, healthy relationship is doing things together, having the trust and comfort to do things apart and always remaining interested in what is happening in each other's lives. We don't live in each other's pockets and don't feel the need to do everything together. We spend time together because we want to, not because we have to or because it is expected of us. We both realise that in order to continue to have things to talk about we need to do things on our own so that at the end of the day we can talk about our experiences and share our stories.

Our relationship is built on mutual trust, something that was sorely lacking between my mother and father but has been passed down to Karen by her parents. We rarely argue, although we do have disagreements from time to time like everyone else. The difference, I've learned since being with Karen, is that things can get sorted if we communicate with each other. I don't regret paying off my mum's mortgage and debts but I now understand why Karen was hurt and I realise I should have discussed it with her first.

A little while ago my mum said I was lucky to have met Karen and she is right, I was! But, after more than 20 years it isn't luck. Most relationships don't last as long as ours. It takes hard work. Karen and I know each other's stories. Other people, when they meet new partners, can recycle a funny story or repeat things that happened in their past before they met. We can't do that because we have been together so long we know each other as well as it is possible to know another human being.

Our relationship lasts because we continually seek out new stories to tell. We listen to what each other has to say. We take time to go out and enjoy things together and make new memories, whether it's walking in a park at sunset holding hands or sharing a joke. As they say, love and laughter are key to a happy ever after.

24
A theatrical car crash

In reimagining the 2,000-year-old wisdom of the great Greek thinker Aristotle, the renowned 20th-century American philosopher William Durant said: 'Success breeds success'. But then he didn't have the pressure of performing for a Glasgow audience on a Saturday night.

While it is undoubtedly true that success can build boldness and self-belief it can also create a painfully sharp double-edged sword. Too little self-assurance can prevent anyone from fulfilling an ambition or reaching a goal, especially if it stops them from even making an attempt. Too much can also prove to be a curse, particularly if it blinds you to potential pitfalls and results in spectacular failure.

Indeed, there have been several academic studies over the years which have clearly demonstrated how initial high achievements can do more harm than good. One classic 1975 Harvard experiment showed how early successes can all too easily lead to overconfidence.

Professor Ellen Langer carried out a simple psychology test in which she split a bunch of students into three groups and asked them to guess heads or tails in a series of coin tosses. Each group was told, rather than shown, if they had guessed correctly or not – and that was key to the experiment.

One group was given the correct result each time they guessed, while another was manipulated into thinking they were right more often at the start of the experiment. The third group was told they had guessed more correctly towards the end of the series of coin flips.

The students were then all asked a series of questions relating to whether they thought they were good at guessing, if they felt that with practice they could improve their skill at predicting the result, or if they believed they had a talent for getting it right.

Once the findings were reviewed it was found the students in the first group, who had been told the correct answers, and those in the third group, who had been led to believe they guessed more accurately near the end of the test, tended to play down any idea they had a skill or special ability to predict the results. However, the students who had been told their early predictions were more often right than wrong were much more likely to think they could beat the 50/50 odds of guessing heads or tails.

In their findings the researchers said the early successes had introduced the idea that there was some skill other than pure chance involved in the task. Many of the students in the third group 'over-remembered past successes and expected more future successes than the other two groups. Involvement had the effect of increasing expectations of future successes and tended to increase their evaluation of their past performance.'

Just as those students had over-imagined their ability to attract success, I was, with the benefit of hindsight, guilty of a little self-deception.

Reeling from the triumph of *Billy & Tim* I thought I had discovered the Midas touch when it came to producing plays. I firmly believed my next venture, another comedy by Des Dillon, would be just as successful and I'd soon have two theatrical hits to enhance my name and my bank balance. The same writer, the same producer and the same marketing strategy, what could possibly go wrong?

Billy & Tim had taught me a lot about marketing, much of it learned more by luck than judgement. When the Citizens Theatre first approached me about putting on the show with them I didn't have any real understanding of the terminology or details of the offer being made. I just kept saying 'no' until I sensed the woman I was talking with was running out of patience. Only then did I say 'yes'. Years later when I had a chance meeting with her she told me I was one of the toughest negotiators she had ever had to deal with. It's amazing what a little bluff and bluster can achieve!

When I decided to produce the *Blue Hen* I was provided with another valuable education, this time mostly relating to what not to do when putting on a show.

The play tells the story of two unemployed working-class men, called Paddy and John. They live on a rough housing scheme in Coatbridge and come up with a hare-brained idea to make some money and keep their bellies full. They are going to rear chickens in the back green of their tenement block and sell the eggs.

However, as is often the case with grand plans, life gets in the way, specifically in the shape of the local psychopathic drug dealer. The result is a highly entertaining black comedy which, on paper, should have been every bit as successful as *Billy & Tim*.

Initially, I had no intention of appearing in the play. I wanted to give others a chance and offered one of the roles to an established Scottish actor who had appeared in a successful television series. Unfortunately, when I approached the Citizens Theatre in Glasgow they refused me the chance to use the large stage unless I secured a 'bigger name' to appear in the play.

Casting my net as wide as possible I managed to attract the attention of veteran actor Charlie Lawson. He was a big name, having appeared in the highly successful, long-running television soap *Coronation Street*. Millions of people watched the show every week and Charlie had been a major character, playing Jim McDonald, for more than a decade.

Charlie had not long finished appearing in the play *Educating Rita* at the Citizens to much acclaim, so it was no surprise when the theatre bosses were delighted that I had managed to sign him for the *Blue Hen*.

The only problem was that Charlie, being so much more established, was going to cost me more than twice as much as I had budgeted. Not only that, but he wanted a four-week rehearsal time rather than the three weeks I had initially planned. The costs of putting on the play began running away from me almost from the get go.

When I set out my plans for the production I had allocated enough money to pay for two actors. However, in order to get the 'big name' the theatre was insisting on I was forced to use my entire budget on Charlie alone. It meant I had to have a very uncomfortable conversation with the young actor I had initially approached and admit I could no longer afford him. I don't think he has ever really forgiven me but, as bad as I felt and still feel to this day, there was nothing else I could do. In order to save the production I had to take the part of the second character. If anyone had to work for free it was going to be me.

In budgeting the production I had also planned to hire a full-time director. Unfortunately the guy I chose for the job wanted to add a further character, called Bannan. Although he only appears in the second half of the play I had to find an extra £500 a week to pay another actor. James McAnerney, who also later went on to appear in *Outlander*, was great in terms of the role but he burst my budget even more.

Just when I thought things couldn't get any worse the director fell out with Charlie on the first day of rehearsal and walked out due to 'artistic differences'. I was suddenly left with no director and no set, as that was supposed to be getting designed by the director. There was no stage lighting design either. I had nothing but a script and three actors and I was worried Charlie was going to walk too. Fortunately, after about the fourth pint, I managed to talk him into staying.

When I told Des Dillon what had happened he offered to come and direct the play with me but the strain of everything was too much and the show failed to live up to my expectations, and those of the theatre critics. To be honest, to borrow the words of *Strictly Come Dancing* judge Craig Revel Horwood: 'It was a complete disaster, darling!'

Thom Dibdin, critic for *The Stage* newspaper, gave it only two stars when he reviewed the press performance, and he openly admitted one of the stars was purely because Charlie Lawson was in it.

When we did get going the ticket sales weren't as good as we had hoped. A mixture of less than favourable reviews along with next to no budget left over for promotion meant the show didn't get the full support it needed to attract enough of an audience.

It wasn't all bad though. Like the curate's egg the play was good in parts. Critic Robert Dawson said, 'The scene, deep into the second half, where the two hopeless layabouts who are our heroes fight off and then truss up a psychotic drug dealer and dump him upside down in a wheelie bin is a gem of black farce.'

Mark Fisher in *The Guardian* likened the *Blue Hen* to the gritty, working-class simplicity and force of 1980s dramas such as *The Boys from the Blackstuff* and compared the script to the works of Alan Bleasdale, John Godber and Willy Russell.

The Times was slightly less complimentary, expressing disappointment that the *Blue Hen* was 'not half as well-made a play' as *Billy & Tim*.

One review of our performance at The Lyceum in Edinburgh started off describing the play as an 'explosion of comedy and pathos that should appeal equally to those who wouldn't normally be seen dead at the Lyceum, as well as to its regular patrons'. It then went on to criticise the set, sound and direction. The only saving grace, thought the author of the review, was for fans of *Coronation Street* to see Charles Lawson, if only 'to witness him succeeding in moving with dignity through what is, otherwise, a theatrical car crash.'

It is a review that sticks in my mind to this day. I think I now understand why the comedian Eric Morecambe used to carry around a review of the first television show he and his partner Ernie Wise did called *Running Wild* in 1954. A damning newspaper review said: 'Definition of the week: TV set – the box in which they buried Morecambe and Wise.' Eric kept it in his wallet as an inspiration to succeed.

There were other issues too that turned out to be very important lessons for me. For a start, Charlie kept ad-libbing things during the performances that hadn't been agreed. I know quite a few actors, especially those with Charlie's level of experience, often do this. They have the ability, honed over years, to read an audience and like to liven things up a bit to keep themselves and the rest of the cast on their toes. Repeating the same lines and actions night after night can get formulaic and sometimes injecting a line or action can create a spark of spontaneity that keeps things fresh, both for the actors and the audience. The trouble was I wasn't as experienced as Charlie and sometimes found it difficult to respond or improvise when he went off script.

There was also one night when we almost set the venue on fire. There is a scene where we had a fake chicken wrapped in a plastic bag. At some point in the play Charlie's character was supposed to produce the chicken but during one performance it was placed too near the stage lights. It started melting and giving off fumes. Without alerting the audience I had to leave my usual mark and improvise a walk across the stage to surreptitiously move it before it caused the fire alarm to go off and force us to evacuate the theatre.

Looking back I think Charlie saw the play as something raw and exciting that he could use as a vehicle to try new things and improvise a little. I, on the other hand, was still too inexperienced and preferred to stick to the script, or at least be warned before the show and given a chance to rehearse any changes he wanted to make.

Getting Charlie was undoubtedly a great coup for me. Here was an actor going from the biggest soap in British television history to working with someone who was little more than a student. Yes, I was putting the show on at a decent theatre but I was still a showbiz newbie. His faith in me meant a lot then and still does.

However, while faith can move mountains, it can't fix everything. I was working a minimum of 14- or 18-hour days doing that show. When you are just one of the actors, especially the star, you can just turn up before the show starts, do your job and then go back to your five-star hotel and relax. I was the one loading and unloading the van, driving the set to each venue on tour, booking the theatres, promoting the show and getting everything ready for each performance. It was exhausting.

Another thing about *Blue Hen* was Charlie and James got paid as the actors, Des got his money as the writer, the theatres made their cut from the sale of the tickets and I, as the producer, ended up with less than nothing. Everybody involved with that show got paid except me. I wasn't taking a wage. I was just bankrolling the whole thing and in the end I was over £22,000 in debt and having sleepless nights.

It just wasn't the right show, the right set or the right time for me. It cost me thousands of pounds in cancelled shows.

As a result of the financial mess of the *Blue Hen* I knew I had to get *Billy & Tim* back on the road to fix my finances. I went to see Colin and James and explained that I didn't have any money but this was my only realistic way of sorting it. Both of them were good enough to say they would wait for their wages until I could get enough cash from the tour to sort out the debt and pay them. It was an incredible show of loyalty and support that I'll never forget.

25

What doesn't kill you makes you stronger

It may be a cliche but the old adage 'what doesn't kill you makes you stronger' has some truth to it. The failure and disappointment of the *Blue Hen* could have ruined my confidence completely and made me want to quit. Instead, it made me even more determined than ever.

Almost over night I found a new energy and threw myself into promoting *Billy & Tim*. I printed tens of thousands of flyers adorned with photos of myself and the rest of cast in our Celtic and Rangers football costumes.

After weeks of plastering my face across the city the extra effort paid off in ways I never expected. Not only did it attract bigger audiences but also the attention of a young woman called Leanne. She had seen my name and photo on one of the flyers and recognised me immediately.

One day, while going through a mountain of emails about the show, I came across a message from her saying she was my wee sister and asking if I would like to meet up.

It was a bolt out of the blue. I was aware my father had remarried and started a new family but I hadn't seen him for 20 years and I had never met my half-siblings.

I knew my mum wouldn't be happy but when I mentioned it to my brother Craig I was a little taken aback at how hostile he was to the idea of renewing any contact. He was dead set against having anything to do with Dad or his second family.

Craig's attitude was very much, 'I've not had a dad all these years so I don't need one now and I don't want to be his mate. I've got enough friends.'

I was more forgiving and I think it's because of all those hours listening to Wayne Dyer on my headset while working nights in the supermarket. It changed my way of thinking.

When Wayne Dyer tried to find his father it was too late, he had already died. Only when he visited his father's grave and let go the anger and bitterness he had stored up over the years was he able to move on. That story had a strong impact on me.

I realised how lucky I was. My father is still alive and I had a chance to speak with him, to find out first-hand what had happened between us. I was ready to embrace this missing part of my life.

I found out later that Craig wasn't the only one with some trepidation about rekindling any contact. My dad had known nothing about Leanne's approach to me. It was weeks after she made the first contact that his wife, Margaret, showed him the poster Leanne had seen. She asked if he recognised the person in the photograph. He didn't. It had been so long since we'd seen each other he didn't know his own son.

When Leanne told him she had been in touch and that I was happy to meet he tried to warn her off. In many ways I could understand his caution. He hadn't seen or spoken with Craig and I for years and had no knowledge of how we had turned out. He was worried we might be bitter or angry and take out any hostility on his new family. After all his last interactions with my mother and her then boyfriend had been less than amicable.

He also didn't know if my mum was still drinking or what I was like. The man my father is now is a far cry from the days when I, aged six, had last seen him. Margaret has been a positive influence on his life. He rarely drinks now, except for the occasional beer at a wedding or occasional night out. He doesn't like to be around drunk people.

However, after several weeks of contact between myself and Leanne he was grudgingly convinced to meet and I invited them all to come to see *Billy & Tim* at the SEC.

My dad was especially reluctant as he knew my mother would be there and feared there could be a scene which would embarrass me and everyone else. Also, he told me later, he didn't want anyone thinking that now I was apparently gaining some success he suddenly wanted to get back in my life.

As it turned out the night they were all due to come and see the show was the same evening Des Dillon told me he was cancelling the agreement for me to produce *Billy & Tim*. It was like something out of a comedy drama. I had arranged a great after-show party. When I got there Craig was drinking too much due to nerves at the thought of meeting Dad again. My mother was struggling with the prospect of having to face her ex-husband and his new wife. All this was going on as I had to pretend everything was okay while concealing my heartbreak over losing the show.

Our first meeting as a family wasn't exactly the night I had envisioned, or spent years as a kid wishing for, but it turned out alright in the end.

I began meeting up occasionally with my newfound siblings and whenever I was short of a player for five-a-side football I'd give my younger brother Steven a call.

It was a very strange feeling to watch somebody I didn't know run like me, play football like me, and have the same movements and mannerisms as me.

It's a weird thing to meet strangers who are your brother and sisters but yet you know nothing about them. I didn't realise how much of gap there had been in my life until I was reunited with them and got to know what I had been missing.

Not only did I discover I had an extra brother and three sisters but that I am an uncle several times over. Leanne has four kids and has something of the same temperament and entrepreneurial spirit I do. Lindsay is into musical theatre and has become a nurse. Steven has two daughters, one of whom is really into acting. It feels crazy that even though we never met until we were adults we share a lot of the same interests and passions.

My sister Debbie is the only one who doesn't seem to have a touch of the show gene. She's much more grounded and is a professional bookbinder, one of only a handful of people in the country that can take old books and rebind them.

26

When one door closes, another opens

'When one door closes, another opens,' a favoured saying of one of my friends, a wise man but a terrible cabinet maker! It's an old joke but as they say, many a truth is said in jest. And, so it was that as one chapter of my life closed with the end of *Billy & Tim* another opened up into a much bigger world – movies.

I wasn't entirely new to filming as I had played a low-level gangster called Kenny McFadden in a six-part Glasgow-based crime series called *The Crews*, which had received limited exposure late at night on local Scottish television.

But, in 2012 I got my first real taste of cinema-style movie making when I got a call to audition for BAFTA-winning director, Ken Loach.

Ken is one of Britain's best film directors having made the classics *Kes*, *The Wind That Shakes the Barley*, *Route Irish*, *Looking for Eric*, *I Daniel Blake* and *Sweet Sixteen* – which launched the career of Martin Compston.

He was in the process of casting for his latest project, *The Angels' Share*, a heart-warming comedy about a group of Glasgow neds who hatch a plot to steal some highly expensive whisky from a distillery.

The angels' share is a term used by whisky distillers to explain the amount of spirit lost to evaporation when the liquid is stored in porous oak barrels for a minimum of three years or more. It's calculated that between 1 and 2 per cent of the volume of a cask is lost each year through evaporation, or as whisky lovers would have us believe is drunk by the angels.

Paul Brannigan, a fellow Weegie lad who had been brought up on the working-class streets of the city, was cast as the main character in the film and Ken was looking for other Glasgow actors to join the cast.

As a result of the success of *Billy & Tim*, and my winning the Best Actor Award at the Edinburgh Fringe, I secured representation from the theatrical agents Lovett Logan Associates. They got me in for an audition for *The Angels' Share* in front of Ken Loach and Kathleen Crawford, who incidentally is the wife of Steven Cree who was also in *Outlander*.

When I went to the audition I was given a series of improvisations alongside Daniel Portman, who went on to star in *Game of Thrones*. The first scenario revolved around Daniel sleeping with my girlfriend and I had to confront him.

I went up to Daniel and said: 'Are you sleeping with my missus?' Daniel said 'Aye', so I grabbed him as though I was going to hit him… and that was the end of the scene. It couldn't really go anywhere after that. In real life characters like the one I was playing would just batter somebody if they admitted sleeping with their wife or girlfriend.

Thankfully Ken gave us another chance. He swapped out Daniel and brought in another guy, Neil Leiper, and switched us around. Neil had to confront me but instead of just saying 'Aye', I denied the affair and tried to protest my 'innocence'. This meant we had something to play with and the scene escalated between the two of us as we concocted a complete story around my trying to explain what had happened, that it was all innocent, and him having to accept that maybe his wife was upset because he wasn't being a good partner or dad to their kids.

Neil is a fantastic actor and we both played the scene for all it was worth. Whatever we did it worked because we both ended up with roles in the film, even though I was stunned when I eventually got the call.

I really didn't expect to get the job as I was up against so many other talented actors. Indeed, I was so convinced I wouldn't get a call back that I went ahead with dental treatment that had been planned for months and got white metal braces fitted to my teeth.

Three weeks later, to my great surprise, I was asked to play Clancy, one of the main villains of the movie. My character was a rival to Paul Brannigan's and a bully. As soon as

I showed up for rehearsal I was told I couldn't play a convincing hard man with braces so the film company paid for me to have them removed and replaced again when filming was all over.

Being forced to go through unnecessary dental treatment was bad enough but when I arrived on set to meet the rest of the cast my heart sank. I remember thinking 'Oh no!' as I was introduced to other members of the cast. One of my fellow actors was related to one of the boys involved in the court case my brother Craig was forced to give evidence in.

Inevitably actors will get together and swap stories of where they are from and I knew that as soon as I said my name and hometown of Rutherglen connections would be made. I didn't know what the reaction might be. This was the biggest moment in my career at that time and I was probably more nervous about that coming up than I was about my part in the movie.

It was a lesson for me that things that happen in your past never get completely forgotten. There is always baggage or something that can come back to haunt you – even years later. As it turned out everything was ok between us.

The first day of filming was one of the opening scenes of the movie. It is set in Glasgow's Sheriff Court and involves my character Clancy and his pals being ejected from the court for disrupting proceedings against the hero of the story, Paul Brannigan, as he is being sentenced for some petty crime. It was a weird experience for me as the court we were using was the actual one I had sat in when we thought my brother would have to give evidence. It felt very strange to be back in there.

Almost as soon as production of the movie got underway, it suddenly stopped. We were getting our make-up and hair done when news came through that filming had been cancelled for the day. We weren't told why just that it was cancelled and we should go home until further notice.

Only much later did we find out that Ken had been going to get something to eat from the food truck when he missed his step, fell and hit his head. The movie shoot which had initially been scheduled to last four weeks was delayed for three months.

Shamefully, I remember thinking 'just my luck to get a role in a Ken Loach movie and before filming starts he goes and dies'. But, I wasn't the only one who thought that. Months later, when filming started again, I confessed my initial fears to some of the other cast members and crew while we were in make-up and quite a few admitted a similar thought had crossed their minds.

I learned a lot working with Ken Loach. The techniques he used on set to get the best out of people were second to none. I often use many of the improvisational techniques he taught us in my drama classes when teaching the next generation of actors. It's nice to be able to pass those skills on.

One very valuable lesson he taught me was that you have to be ready for anything. Ken never released a script to the cast before we arrived on set. It meant we never really knew what to expect day to day. Normally, in most other projects I've been involved with the cast are informed in advance what scenes are to be filmed so they learn their lines before arriving on set.

However, it did mean the entire cast was free, up to a point, to improvise on set each day and that made for a fun and exciting experience, albeit sometimes surprising.

There is a scene in the film in which Paul's character ambushes his rival, Clancy, in the tanning salon. When I turned up for the shoot all I knew was that we'd be filming a scene in a sun bed shop. Nobody told me until just before the cameras started rolling that I would have to be naked in the scene.

For more than 12 hours I had to hang about with my bits out as we did several takes only to discover when the film was eventually released that it hadn't made the final cut. You only really see me from the neck up.

When I met Ken at the after party for the film premiere I asked why the nude scene had been scrapped. It was meant to have been one of the final scenes of the film but Ken said after some reflection it was decided it would have put a totally different spin on the movie. Although it was one of my favourite scenes to film I understood straight away what Ken meant.

Like all good screen baddies the role of Clancy was fun to play. I was able to base his mannerisms and attitude on scores of people I had grown up alongside. The braggart swagger, aggressive puffing out of his chest, waving of the arms, dancing around on the balls of the feet like a bad boxer and the chicken-like forward jerks of the head were all movements I had witnessed lads doing as they squared up to each other in the streets.

I remember the late, great actor James Cagney telling a talk-show host how he got his trademark stiff-legged, trouser-hitching, shoulder-rolling, cuff-pulling actions. They were accompanied by a click of the fingers and hitting of the palm of his left hand off the top of his clenched fist, before raising his hand up to hip level with his fingers forming the shape of a gun.

It's a series of gestures mimicked by generations of impressionists and comedians, especially the likes of Frank Gorshan, as they say the immortal line, 'You dirty rat!' A line which, incidentally, Cagney never said in any of his films.

Cagney said that as a boy, aged about 12, he used to watch from his window a man in a sharp suit and fedora hat across the street. The man spent the whole day on the sidewalk at the corner of 78th Street and 1st Avenue in New York making these peculiar movements to hail acquaintances as if he was a big shot, a man of importance.

According to Cagney it was all the man ever did, all day, every day. He never seemed to work for a living. Even when somebody would walk past and greet him the man never said anything, he just shrugged his shoulders and went through his routine.

When Cagney was cast as Rocky Sullivan in the classic 1938 movie *Angels with Dirty Faces* he remembered the guy on the street corner and introduced some of the mannerisms into the character, and it was a big hit. Cagney won Best Actor from the National Board of Review and the New York Film Critics Circle as well as being nominated for the Best Actor Oscar in the 1939 Academy Awards.

Actors spend a lot of time observing others, how they speak move or act. Sometimes we don't realise we are doing it but then get called for a part and suddenly remember something somebody did that fits perfectly. You never know when you are going to see a gesture, involuntary tick or hear a phrase or accent that can be used at a later date to bring a character to life and tell a story.

I got the walk that Clancy does in the film from a boy that used to live close to us. He walked with a swing so exaggerated it appeared as if he was always checking to see if an imaginary parrot was still perched on his shoulder. He clearly thought it was the walk of a hard man. Those of us who knew him thought it was more amusing than scary, although nobody ever said that to his face.

On the day where I was supposed to be doing my biggest scene in the movie things went terribly wrong. It involved me running down the street chasing after Paul, the main star of the film. It was a big operation, they had to close off the street for a day and bring in lots of background actors and all the crew to film this one scene.

During one of the first takes a woman, an ordinary member of the public, passing by thought it was real and heroically tried to intervene to save Paul. The shoot had to be stopped and started all over again, and that's when disaster really struck.

As soon as Ken shouted action I started to run down the street after Paul and really began to build up some speed when suddenly I heard a sharp pop and a searing pain shot through my leg. I had snapped a hamstring.

I guess I hadn't warmed up properly and had tried to go from a cold standing start to full sprint. As soon as it happened I thought my film acting career was over, not because of the injury as I knew that would mend but because they had to cancel the whole day's shoot. Everybody was sent home with full pay and incredibly expensive production time was lost.

It's ironic that I've never had an injury playing football or anything but on this day of all days it had to happen. The pain was excruciating but nothing like the embarrassment I felt that the whole shoot had to be cancelled.

The film company paid for my medical treatment, including having to go to Hampden football stadium for state-of-the-art physio using ultraviolet light and stuff like that. It was six weeks before my injury healed and they could reschedule.

When we eventually managed to reorganise the shoot I was worried everyone would be mad at me but it was the reverse. Shooting had wrapped on the rest of the film so it was like a reunion with everyone getting back together for this one day. Instead of being fed up all the cast and crew involved were delighted to be getting another day's wage out of the film.

The next time we all got together was the premiere and the party afterwards at the Arches, though I almost missed it. The PR and marketing team had sent out the invitations and the party tickets were designed to look like beer mats.

I didn't realise and my mum had taken them and stuck them in her scrapbook. When Karen and I turned up for the party at the Arches the doorman wouldn't let me in without a ticket. I felt gutted. This was my first movie and I couldn't get in. Karen and I had to stand there and watch all the members of the cast and crew walk past us. Eventually the doorman relented and let us enter.

That was probably the last time everyone was able to be themselves. Whenever we tried to meet up after that it never felt the same, there was a different vibe.

When we did the film we were all just people off the schemes. None of us had experienced any brush with fame. Even though we each had various levels of acting experience, in between roles we had to make a living. William Ruane was a window cleaner. He ended up selling his round to my brother Steven. Gary Maitland, who played the nerdy guy in the movie who has the immortal line, 'Is that Edinburgh Castle up there?', was a bin cleaner. I had been doing a variety of jobs. We were all just very ordinary folk.

Once the film went on general release and been a success for a while we'd all had experiences with the paparazzi, been VIP'd and recognised in the street by fans of the film. It changed the dynamic and a hierarchy of sorts began to creep in. It's human nature I guess but things were never quite the same again. A similar sort of thing happened on *Outlander* once the show really began to take off.

The film itself was well received by the critics and the public. It was nominated for the Magritte Award for Best Foreign Film in Coproduction, won the prestigious Jury Prize at the 2012 Cannes Film Festival and scooped more than £4 million at the box office.

Getting *The Angels' Share* was a major trigger point for me. Before getting a part in that movie I was Scott from the scheme, after appearing in the film I was Scott the actor.

27

A great British tradition

After my dental and hamstring comedy of errors in the making of *The Angels' Share*, along with the self-inflicted farce of the *Blue Hen*, it seemed only natural that pantomime should play a large part in the next stage of my career.

As with a lot of opportunities that have presented themselves over the years the chance to produce a pantomime came out of the blue, and it was one I seized with both hands.

The traditional Christmas panto is often looked down upon by some theatre goers, especially those who feel it is intellectually inferior or have lost the ability to relive the feelings of innocent youthful exuberance. But, as is often the case, the truth is very different.

The origins of this great British tradition can be traced back to the age of classical theatre, performed on the hillsides of Greece or in the amphitheatres of Rome. Combine it with a little commedia dell'arte from 16th-century Italy, a pinch of double entendre, a dash of English music hall ribaldry and a bucket of slapstick and you have the makings of a laughter-inducing cocktail of fun that has delighted audiences across the four nations for more than 150 years.

Despite the multi-cultural influences that have helped create such a unique genre of live entertainment it is really only in the UK that it has become something of a national treasure, an essential part of the winter festivities that attracts more than three million people a year to the theatre.

Scotland in particular has embraced the pantomime vigorously, and many of the nation's most legendary comics and actors have helped develop the art into the type of shows most people would recognise today as a 'traditional panto'.

Scottish greats such as Stanley Baxter, Harry Gordon, Jack Milroy, Angus Lennie, Gerard Kelly, Mary Lee, Elaine C Smith, Johnny Beattie, Gregor Fisher, Rikki Fulton, Will Fyffe, and Dave Willis among many others have all taken to the panto stage, injecting their brand of humour and comedy into the roles.

It was in Scotland that the idea of the Dame, a man dressed up as a woman to play a lusty widow, first materialised as comics of the day realised there was a big laugh to be had from watching a butch bloke in a frock.

It was also in Scotland that the art of addressing the audience directly with a crafty aside from the footlights and lacing the script with topical or hometown gags to delight the local crowd and make them feel a part of the show, began.

Colour and spectacle are every bit as important as the script and the acting, especially for youngsters who are easily mesmerised by the magic of dancing lights and sparkling glitter.

I've often wondered if one of the reasons panto remains so popular in Scotland, apart from it being a show every generation of a family can enjoy together, is that it is essentially moral. Good always wins over bad and the underdog, usually the common man, gets one over on the tyrannical villain. It's pretty much a comic depiction of the working-class fantasy.

Panto is a cornerstone of the arts. It is maybe the only time in a year that so many people go to see a live performance. As a result many theatres rely on the annual pantomime to subsidise everything else they do; unsurprisingly, it is big business and is taken very seriously.

Following the success I'd had with *Billy & Tim* I was asked to produce the pantomime at my local venue, Rutherglen Town Hall. As with so many opportunities that have come my way this also arose by accident.

I had gone to see if there were any dates left I could book for a new *Billy & Tim* tour. While I was chatting with the theatre manager he said it was a pity we didn't do pantomimes as *Billy & Tim* had been such a success. Without hesitating I immediately said, 'Of course we do pantomimes, we are a theatre company.'

Up until this point in my life I had only been involved with student panto during my college years and probably didn't fully appreciate the ordeal I was talking myself into.

Right there, on the spot, the manager asked if my company, NLP, could produce their version of *Cinderella*. The people they had been using previously had been paid about £7,000 for producing the panto and ticket sales were only around £10,000, so there was very little profit in it for the theatre. He obviously hoped I could pull off something similar to my success with *Billy & Tim*.

In the space of a couple of hours I went from being the producer of one show, *Billy & Tim*, to putting on my first professional pantomime. Once again I found myself working with a shoestring budget and had to call in a lot of favours if I was going to have any chance of making it work.

Although pantomimes may appear chaotic and spontaneous they take a lot of planning and rehearsing. Making something look easy usually involves a lot of hard work.

A good panto is like a cordon bleu meal in a five-star Michelin restaurant. The experience for the consumer is magical but they never get to see the mental, emotional and physical stress that goes on behind the scenes to create the finished dish.

Although each pantomime is different there is a tried and tested formula which is, in essence, a celebration of old-fashioned bawdiness in the best carry-on camping-it-up tradition. The dame, a garishly made-up character with overdeveloped false breasts, padded derrière and a dress sense so ludicrous as to make the most outrageous cat-walk fashion designer envious, is central.

Tradition dictates there should be a cloak swirling, hand-rubbing, moustache-twirling like villain, who superstitiously always enters the stage from the left. The baddie is usually served by at least one or preferably two sidekicks so intellectually challenged as to be potential political candidates.

Audience participation plays a big part. Children and adults alike are encouraged to boo the baddies and shout out catchphrases of the favourite characters.

There also has to be a romantic element of sorts with a good-looking couple who go through the machinations of a love that is found, lost and found again in time for the finale.

Casting a panto is a delicate task. Theatres want familiar faces and big names to attract the crowd but that means higher production costs. Unfortunately, just because someone is a 'weel kent face', it doesn't mean they will be any good.

Not everyone is suited for pantomime but for those who rise to the challenge it provides seasonal employment for a myriad of performers from across many showbiz genres. Seasoned pop stars, retired athletes and legendary comedians rub shoulders, or lamps, alongside jobbing actors and drama students just starting out on the climb up the grease-painted pole to fame and fortune.

Panto is hard work. It requires a lot of stamina and dedication to perform the same lines show after show with all the frantic costume changes, dance routines and physical comedy six days a week for around three to four months at a time in front of a live audience.

Behind the scenes getting everything organised, sets designed, props acquired, costumes made and a diverse cast of varying experience up to speed, and tickets sold within a very short timescale is a Herculean challenge for every director and producer.

The cost of putting on a panto is not cheap either. In addition to the wages for the cast and crew there's the cost of costumes, set designs, prop hire, marketing, theatre commissions and a host of other expenses which make every production a gamble. If all goes well and tickets sell then a theatre can make more than half its annual profits in a matter of weeks. If things go wrong the losses can be horrific.

In agreeing to put on the Rutherglen panto I was aware of many of the challenges ahead but not necessarily fully appreciative of them. But, once again, I got lucky.

Among my first hires were Kevin Mains, who played the priest in *Outlander* who officiates the wedding of the two main characters, and Chris Forbes, best known for *Scot Squad*. They played the Ugly Sisters in our version of *Cinderella*. For budget reasons primarily I played the dame, but Kevin and Chris stole the show.

In order to cut costs I managed to borrow some costumes from the Citizens Theatre and we reused the set from *Blue Hen*, after repainting it to show a scene for *Cinderella*. Hop Scotch Theatre gave us some props and we picked the rest up from pound stores and charity shops.

Thankfully the show was a triumph and NLP managed to double the sales on the previous Christmas, much to the delight of the theatre manager who immediately hired us for a production of *Aladdin* the following year.

As word of our success at Rutherglen got out I was approached by the Byer Theatre in St Andrews and asked to stage a version of *Aladdin* for them.

Again I was fortunate to get a good cast, including Richard Rankin, who has since found great fame in *Outlander* as Roger MacKenzie, and the lead role in the latest TV adaptations of the Inspector Rebus books.

Using some of the marketing techniques I had developed to promote *Billy & Tim*, NLP's pantomimes did well. At one point I had shows in six theatres across the country running simultaneously.

The responsibility of putting on so many pantomimes at the same time was financially hugely stressful. For a start, I quickly discovered very few theatres, especially ones run by local authority councils, were prepared to put any money up front against projected ticket sales. That meant I had to fund the shows in their entirety until income from sales had come in and been counted. In most circumstances that could take weeks, long after the run had finished.

Fortunately Karen and her mum were willing to invest so we could get the pantomimes off the ground. They paid production costs and the actors' wages.

Pantomime was an excellent education in more ways than one. Not only did I get to see a range of human behaviour I also became acutely aware of the risks of mixing politics and entertainment.

One of the attractions of panto is its ability to poke fun at establishment figures and insert topical gags tailor-made to appeal to specific audiences.

During one production of *Jack and the Beanstalk* at Rutherglen Town Hall we were forced to cut a joke about Margaret Thatcher from the show because theatre bosses deemed it too political.

Cast member and comedian Raymond Mearns called the pantomime cow in the show Thatcher – because it didn't produce milk for the children. The audience thought it was hilarious but the council deemed it inappropriate, even though there had been no complaints.

The story went viral on social media and made headlines in the local press. Despite the minor inconvenience of having to change the name of the character the boost in publicity resulted, in the best traditions of panto, in a happy ending all round.

28

Necessity is the
mother of invention

Following on from my pantomime productions I made my first foray into theatre management. And boy, what an eye-opener that was!

Producing a play, or even several pantos at a time, can be a physical, mental and emotional challenge but it's a walk in the park compared to the machinations of managing a successful venue.

A good theatre manager is a jack of all trades but, unlike the old proverb, he cannot afford to be a master of none. He has to be a maestro of several arts, and some much darker than you might imagine.

It is a job that requires no real formal qualifications but rather a smorgasbord of skills and experience, usually only acquired after some on-the-job training using the sink or swim method of learning.

Administrating the day-to-day operations of any kind of performing arts centre calls for at least some understanding of business, communications, planning, finance, and marketing.

And, if that's not enough, you also need to be good at dealing with people, understanding health and safety, providing leadership, being adept at diplomacy, and to have the strength of character to avoid getting embroiled in 'office politics'. It's a lot to take on and, unsurprisingly, these skills take time to learn. Being a theatre manager can be hugely enjoyable but also deeply frustrating. Trust me!

My first foray into the backstage world of theatre management came, like many of my career crossroads, out of the blue. I was touring with one of my pantomimes when I was approached by the chairman of The Regal Community Theatre in Bathgate.

Possibly as a result of the success garnered by both *Billy & Tim* and the pantos, due to my sometimes unorthodox marketing methods, he asked if I would consider speaking at a meeting to help try and bolster the fortunes of the struggling Regal Theatre.

The historic 1930s Art Deco venue underwent a dramatic nine-month restoration in 2010 and the newly transformed venue had ambitions to become one of the best arts venues in central Scotland. But, to do that they needed to raise the theatre profile and increase audience attendance.

I can't remember what I said at that meeting but it must have impressed somebody because I was offered a two days a week contract for nine months, with no budget, to try and turn the theatre around.

They say 'naivety is a fool's blessing' and 'necessity is the mother of invention' – both of these could equally apply to my decision in 2012 to accept the offer to become the Artistic Director of The Regal Theatre.

I have long been in agreement with the quote from actress and Hollywood icon Julie Andrews who said: 'The arts bridge cultures; they're good for the economy, and they're good for fostering empathy and decency.' That's exactly what The Regal stood for and I couldn't wait to get involved.

As with almost all community theatres and arts venues funding is an ongoing challenge. One of my many tasks was to promote the theatre to a wider population and improve box office receipts.

As a novice to the world of theatre management I was unfamiliar with the usually accepted conventions of 'how things are supposed to be done', specifically when it comes to funding in the arts. I'd never relied on grants, donations or benefactors to finance my work in the past so, in retrospect, I may have ruffled a few feathers with my different approach to income generation.

Almost immediately I set about an expansive marketing campaign to attract new productions. I paid £9,000 out of my own pocket to create banners, publish brochures and fund leaflet drops in residential neighbourhoods to encourage more people to come to the theatre, many of them for the first time.

I did it because I knew that with only three years of college and limited professional acting experience there was no other way I was going to get a job managing a theatre. It was an opportunity and I was determined to succeed.

Many of the hours I put into organising open days and fundraising galas, producing merchandise and attracting media coverage were done unpaid, over and above my contracted time. Within a few years The Regal Community Theatre posted a profit for the first time in its history. We more than doubled box office sales, increased bar profits and became one of the busiest and most talked about theatres in the country.

It was a rollercoaster ride that was supposed to last just nine months but ended up being five years. One of my highlights was working with Susan Boyle, a local West Lothian resident of the area.

Susan is a remarkable talent and a very humble person. She shot to fame in 2009 on the third season of the television talent show *Britain's Got Talent*. Anyone who has seen that performance won't forget how this unassuming 48-year-old stunned the world with her performance of the song 'I Dreamed a Dream' from the musical *Les Miserables*. It remains one of the more memorable auditions in the history of the show, and most watched performances on YouTube.

Susan has been involved with The Regal for many years and during my time there became an official patron. As a public face of the theatre she has done much to inspire youngsters, even joining in classes with students to help and support them.

My own fundraising attempts for the theatre were given an extra boost after my appearance on *Outlander*. Among the many friends I made on the show was Stephen Walters and he was the one who suggested that I sign up for a Twitter account, or X as it is now known.

I started with four followers, including Stephen, and I followed them back. I made a point of reciprocating whenever anyone followed me; I couldn't believe why *Outlander* fans would be interested in the guy who gets the horses on the show.

To my amazement, within little more than a year, I got to 122,000 followers, and they turned out to be very supportive and generous.

One day, while stuck in a traffic jam, I posted a silly little video on X. I can't even remember what it was about but suddenly a lot of people started asking about the T-shirt I was wearing in the video. It was part of my uniform for the theatre but people liked it and wanted to buy one.

Sensing an opportunity I called the theatre and asked for a link to be put up on the website advertising the T-shirts for sale. That quickly led to a range of merchandise, including teddy bears, caps, hoodies and much more.

All the profits went directly to the Bathgate Regal fund. Combined with donations to the theatre's JustGiving page and various events, we raised more than £80,000 in the space of a few months.

The hard work paid off. Our entrepreneurial approach to promotion led to the town of Bathgate being nominated for a Creative Places Award in 2015, and I was presented with the 'Pride of West Lothian' Award in 2017 in 'special recognition for outstanding contribution to The Bathgate Regal Community Theatre and West Lothian'.

29

Type cast

When I look back at my stage career I sometimes wonder if there is a pattern to some of the roles I get offered, or whether I'm just naturally attracted to those parts because of my background.

A lot of the plays I've done have involved gang violence, mental health issues, drug addiction, racism, sectarianism and war. Although many of these productions have dealt with such important issues with a touch of humour, they are still pretty much taboo topics in polite society.

The first such play I did was *Cold Turkey at Nana's* back in 2012 at Glasgow's legendary Oran Mor. Described as a 'wry, funny and sharp' play it was still all about drug addiction.

My role was that of Tony, a young man who slowly transforms from a drug-driven demon to something approaching a decent human being. It got rave reviews and somehow set me on a path of telling darker kinds of stories.

Even when I joined the Charioteer Theatre Company to do a play called *Gang*, directed by Laura Pasetti, and toured Italy with it, I was cast as a boy from the slums who joins a gang.

The play may have been inspired by Homer's *Iliad* but its depiction of teenage knife culture felt all too familiar to me, a boy who grew up in Glasgow during the 1990s. Maybe it was that closeness to reality which helped me and the others to put on a performance the critics described as 'must see' for the feelings of 'anger, desperation and sadness' emitted by the characters.

Violence and its disastrous consequences are a big part of the play and having lived through some of that, and seen the real thing impact others first-hand, it did feel a little too close to home sometimes.

Laura Pasetti turned out to be a major influence on my career. I spent two years working with her in Italy, learning about preparation and performance. As a result I credit her with my Stage Best Actor Award (2010) at the Edinburgh Fringe.

At some point in life we will all meet a Laura, the trick is recognising it. I learn from everyone I work with, whether they are my peers, fresh faces or old hands but often the best lessons come from unexpected sources.

After *Gang* came more plays exploring similar themes, including the role of Eddie in a Finnish play called *Bad Boy Eddie* written by Anna Krogerus. But, it was possibly playing a young drug addict in *One Mississippi*, a play about male suicide, that was the most rewarding.

It tells the stories of a group of four men with histories of mental distress, substance abuse and suicidal thoughts. It is based on extensive real-life interviews with two guys from Glasgow, one from Belfast and one from Edinburgh about how the impact of childhood experiences can shape adult lives.

One Mississippi is an extraordinary piece of verbatim theatre, directed by my old friend Umar Ahmed, so I jumped at the chance to join the cast when the role was offered.

Umar and I went to college together almost two decades ago and we have been great friends ever since. He came to my wedding in Cyprus and I attended his a few years later.

We had worked together before, in 2013, when we produced *How to Make a Killing in Bollywood* which toured the UK and played to sold out audiences at the Edinburgh Festival. I knew that with him at the helm the play would be a success.

In some ways I was luckier than other members of the cast because I got to see the man behind the character I was playing. The people whose words we were using were meant to be anonymous but when he saw the way I was portraying him during rehearsals he came forward and introduced himself. He was another guy called Tony.

He thought I was nailing his character and after chatting a while I realised why. Tony was brought up just a few streets from me in Toryglen. I know the area well, I used to walk through it to go to my granny's house.

His life was one I could relate to in so many ways. We knew a lot of the same people. Our backgrounds were so similar but we just happened to take different paths. He grew up turning to drink and drugs, eventually becoming a heroin addict, while I went into acting, and ended up playing fictional characters mirroring his reality.

In many ways playing Tony in *One Mississippi* felt easier because we were of the same time. One role I found a little more challenging and a lot more heartbreaking was that of Annan Ness in *A War of Two Halves* at the Edinburgh Fringe Festival in 2019.

It is the true story of the Heart of Midlothian players who volunteered for the First World War and it's a highly emotional play.

Superbly written by Paul Beeson and Tim Barrow, it was directed by Bruce Strachan and followed the fortunes of the team as they swapped the pitch at Tynecastle for the trenches of France.

On 25 November 1914, 11 Hearts players enlisted to fight in the First World War. They volunteered in the wake of a media storm that had criticised Britain's professional sportsmen for lacking the enthusiasm shown by thousands of ordinary men who had signed up almost as soon as war broke out in the August.

Critics accused the sportsmen of shirking their responsibilities and the UK government was said to have been on the verge of banning soccer for the duration of the war.

When Edinburgh businessman Lieutenant Colonel Sir George Macrae boasted he could raise a battalion in a week, things changed. But it didn't take him a week. He did it in six days.

Among the 1,347 men who answered Macrae's call were the Heart of Midlothian boys, who at the time were at the top of the Scottish League. They were soon joined by players from other clubs, such as Raith Rovers, Falkirk and Dunfermline, along with hundreds of fans from each club.

Known affectionately as the Sportsman's Battalion, or Macrae's Own, of the 16th Royal Scots regiment the men were sent to France in January 1916 and the slaughter of the Western Front.

At 7.30am on 1 July 1916 a whistle blew and the Sportsmen Battalion climbed out of their trench and walked towards the German line and into Hell.

Within minutes four officers and 225 other ranks were dead. Another six officers and 341 enlisted men were wounded, some of them fatally. A total of 60,000 men were killed or wounded in just a few short hours. It was the bloodiest day in British military history.

After the battle Hearts manager John McCartney received a number of letters from the surviving team members detailing what had happened to their comrades.

Annan Ness, the character I played, wrote of seeing the team's left back Duncan Currie shot in the right shoulder. He also witnessed Harry Wattie, the forward, fall and Pat Crossan, right back, blown up by an artillery shell.

Others were also hit. Teddy McGuire, the inside forward, was wounded in the arm by shrapnel and fell as a machine gun bullet grazed his head. Ernie Ellis, midfield, and Jimmy Hawthorn, former midfield, were both shot as they reached the enemy barbed wire. Jimmy Hazeldean of the youth team took a bullet in the thigh.

As one survivor later wrote poignantly, 'the lads fell like corn before the scythe'.

Another player, Jimmy Boyd, was killed in action a few days later.

As a massive football fan it was a privilege to play Ness. He had been a professional soldier before playing full back for Hearts and it's clear from letters sent home that he was something of a leader for the boys in the trenches.

Ness rose through the ranks to Regimental Sergeant Major before achieving a battlefield commission for his bravery during a rear-guard action near Ypres. Although he survived the war I don't think he ever got over what had happened to his teammates. He died in Edinburgh in 1942 aged just 50.

The play was very cleverly performed in the Tynecastle Stadium as it took the audience from the bar through the turnstiles with a ghost of the old team playing in the pitch, the dressing room and then to the trenches of France.

It was an incredible experience for both the actors and the audience but not my first time in a khaki uniform.

The year previously I was fortunate to be cast in another great play about footballers and soldiers.

The Greater Game, written by Michael Head and directed by Adam Morley, told the tale of how 41 footballers and members of staff of Leyton Orient, or Clapton Orient as they were then known, were the first soccer team to enlist together for the 17th Battalion Middlesex Regiment, affectionally known as the 'Footballers' Battalion', in World War 1.

I played George Scott in this strongly emotive play, which not only deals with loss, as not all the players returned from the war, but also the physical and psychological scars suffered by the survivors.

My character, Scott, was one of three Orient players who never made it back from the war. He was wounded and taken as a prisoner of war but died in a German military hospital on 16 August 1916, aged just 30.

One day I hope I'll be able make a trip to the war cemetery at St Souplet in northern France to lay a flower on his grave and say thank you.

30

Oh, for fuck's sake

Playing a real person from history has its pressures but, as almost any actor will tell you, portraying somebody who is still alive and looking over your shoulder is another level of daunting altogether. Especially when that character turns out to be a real-life hero.

In 2014 I landed a role in *Kajaki: The True Story*, a docudrama which was later released in the USA under the title *Kilo Two Bravo*. Described as a British version of the Oscar-winning *Hurt Locker*, it is no ordinary war movie.

It tells the extraordinary tale of how in September 2006 four anti-personnel mines, left behind by the Soviet occupation of Afghanistan in the 1980s, were accidentally detonated by a British army patrol. One person was killed and seven others seriously wounded.

It all began when Corporal Stuart 'Stu' Pearson and his mates were tasked with protecting the Afghan village of Kajaki from Taliban fighters. From their outpost, codenamed 'Normandy', on a hillside overlooking the valley, they spotted enemy activity below.

In an attempt to get a better position, Lance Corporal Stuart Hale and a few others decided to move to another vantage point and set off across the valley. As they made their way down the hillside L/C Stu Hale stood on a mine. It immediately blew off the lower portion of his right leg and a finger.

Initially the patrol thought it was an ambush and called for support, including a helicopter evacuation for their wounded comrade.

While some of the guys administered first aid to their mate, Stu Pearson slipped on a rock and triggered a second explosion, amputating part of his leg.

Stranded on the floor of the sun-drenched valley, exposed to the searing heat and flies, while all the time in constant danger of enemy attack, the paratroopers had no option but to wait for help.

Unfortunately the only air support available at the time was a twin-bladed Chinook helicopter. It did not have a winch to airlift the wounded and couldn't land because of the danger of more landmines. As it turned out the caution was merited. The powerful downdraft from the chopper set off another explosion, causing even more injuries to the troops on the ground.

Kajaki is not the typical all-action style of war movie but rather a tense, emotionally charged drama. It focuses on the camaraderie and courage shown by a small group of men trapped in a terrifying, dangerous situation that most of us will thankfully never have to endure.

When I first read the script it was very hard to hold back the emotions. It was clear the writer Tom Williams, and everyone behind the movie, had done their research thoroughly. I knew instantly I wanted to be a part of it, and that's often a bad thing for an actor.

Normally you get put forward for a role by your agent, you go to an audition and if you hear back that's great. If you don't get the part then you try to forget about it and move on. But, when you become invested in the idea of the character you want to play there's a lot at stake and rejection is so much harder to handle.

I was asked to read for the role of Sergeant Stuart 'Stu' Pearson and I knew right away it was something I could do. Stu is from East Kilbride, brought up in an area just a short drive from where I was from. Long before I met him I had an idea of what he was like. I had a good understanding of his world. We shared very similar accents, had lived in almost identical neighbourhoods and used the same vocabulary. I had a good idea of how he probably talked, walked and thought.

When I went to London for the audition I was really worried they'd want me to neutralise my accent, Stu's accent, to make it more palatable for a non-Glaswegian audience. I knew in my gut that if they did it would detract from the reality of the character. Fortunately, I needn't have worried.

My agent told me later that as soon as I walked into the room the director said: 'That's Stu Pearson!'

I was delighted when I got the role but that's when the hard work really started. When you are portraying a living person and trying to recreate a dramatic moment in somebody's life there is a lot of pressure to get it right. It's not like playing a fictional character where you have some freedom to invent a personality. But, equally, you are not there to try and do an impersonation or create a caricature. The pressure was nerve-wracking, especially when Stu was ultimately looking over my shoulder.

Before meeting Stu I spent weeks researching his life. I found photos of him online, watched videos of interviews he had given, studied his mannerisms and speech patterns. I read up on the war in Afghanistan and everything I could find about the incident in Kajaki. By the time we did get together Stu said it seemed I knew more about his life than he did.

All of the cast had similar experiences. When we started the journey members of the 3rd Parachute Regiment who knew the real people told us, in no uncertain terms, that we had 'fucking big shoes to fill'. Many were dubious that we, a bunch of actors, could really do justice to what those men did, especially the actions of Corporal Mark Wright who was awarded the George Cross for his bravery.

To be honest the 'big shoes' comment was a massive understatement. None of us could ever really get anywhere near to following in the footsteps of those brave men but we were all determined to do our best in the hope that by telling their story they would at least gain a fraction of the recognition and respect they deserved.

Playing Stu Pearson was undoubtedly one of the most daunting, but rewarding, tasks I've ever faced. Although he would deny it Stu is a real live hero, and he's got the Queen's Gallantry Medal to prove it. What he did and endured as a soldier in Afghanistan is the stuff of nightmares.

Right from the beginning my responsibility was to Stu, his family and friends. I had to play the role as best I could for them. They would watch the film expecting to see the soldier they knew up on that screen, not some unrecognisable fictional character with the same name. It was a heavy responsibility and I knew I had to get it right. Usually actors want to please the movie reviewers and the paying public, but this was different. I cared much more about what Stu, his family and comrades would think than I did of any armchair critic's opinion.

Once all the actors had been cast we were bused off to Colchester, home of 3 Para, to undergo some real military training at the hands of experienced former paratroopers.

It might only have been a couple of days, and a small taste of what the professional soldiers go through, but it was tough. The instructors treated us like real recruits. Any thoughts they might go easy on us because we were actors playing at being in the military were short-lived.

It was important we got the details right, even the minor ones. Something as simple as how to hold our weapons, move in a combat zone or even just carry our rucksacks helped us to create an illusion of authenticity. It also helped us work as a team, become comfortable with the technical language and the way guys in these kinds of situations relate to each other.

During bootcamp, after the day's training finished, I spent a lot of time with Stu and his pals, much of it in the pub. It was an education and a half. These were ordinary guys who had experienced an extraordinary event and who looked after one another in the face of great personal danger and suffering. Their sense of camaraderie was a masterclass in selflessness and humility, albeit with a little black humour thrown in.

Stu told me that after he had lost his leg and been evacuated to a military hospital his pals came to visit. To cheer him up they brought him an eye patch, a toy parrot for his shoulder and a running magazine.

As an outsider to this intimate little group it took some time to break down the understandable emotional barriers before Stu began to really open up. The breakthrough moment happened at 6am one morning, after numerous beers had been consumed during a long lock in session in a Colchester pub. We'd both had a fair bit to drink so it seemed easier to ask some of the more difficult questions that might have felt awkward or even ghoulishly voyeuristic if we had been sober. I remember asking things like, 'How did you feel when you stepped on the mine?' 'What was going through your mind?' 'Did you think you would die?' They were very personal questions but in order to try and get inside his head, understand his character and get it right, I felt they were necessary.

To my surprise, and slight disappointment, Stu's answers were almost clinical in their detail. He described how he had cleared a path and was retracing his steps to show his colleagues the route was clear when a rock he had stepped on slipped and his foot landed on a mine.

Calmly he told me how the explosion sent him hurtling into the air and as he crashed down into the dust he said to himself, 'Oh, for fuck's sake!' There was no terror or panic in the way he described his reaction, it was if he had knocked over his beer or a cup of coffee rather than having had his lower leg blown off.

When Stu told me his training immediately kicked in and that he quickly reached for his morphine capsule, injected it into his leg, and tried to deal with the wound himself, I was thinking about how I would depict that in the film. The way Stu told the story there was no drama, it was all textbook first aid treatment. As an actor, I thought it wasn't going to be much of a scene in the movie.

However, fast forward a couple of days and we're back in the pub with all his mates and they're asking me how it was going. When I said what Stu had told me about his training kicking in, administering the morphine to himself and all the other stuff, they all started laughing.

'Did he fuck,' said one of the paras who had been there when the mine went off. 'He was screaming for his mammy and making a hell of a racket. He doesn't remember, he was in shock. He thinks he did all that stuff he told you but he didn't.'

It may seem odd but hearing those words from Stu's friends was a bit of a relief for me, there was some artistic license to play with. Now I knew exactly how I was going to play the scene.

Filming took place in the Jordanian desert, a safer substitute for the hills of Afghanistan. It had been due to start shortly after boot camp but for various reasons was delayed a few weeks so by the time we arrived in Jordan it was brutally hot.

At times the temperature was 58°c or more. It got so warm that at least two of the crew's thermometers broke and there was a real concern that the heat could damage the camera equipment and put an end to filming.

We really fried in the heat. I don't know how much factor 50 I used but it must have been gallons of the stuff. After just 15 seconds in the sun you'd be drenched in sweat. There were days when I had to lie in the dirt, with my lower leg buried in the sand to mimic Stu's wound, for up to 12 hours at a time.

Working in that burning desert certainly added to the authenticity. It made us think about what it must have been like, stuck in a minefield in the middle of a combat zone with no idea when help might come. I don't think any of our performances would have been as good if we'd been sitting in a studio backlot in the UK or in front of a green screen.

On the day we were due to film the explosion in which Stu lost his leg, I didn't tell the rest of the cast what I had in mind. I wanted to see how they reacted. I walked into the minefield just as Stu had done, I stepped on the rock as he did and then there was an explosion. When it came to filming my closeup, supposedly right after the dust had cleared, I repeated the line, 'Oh, for fuck's sake!' Up until that moment it was just as Stu had remembered, but then I let rip.

I screamed for morphine and when the other guys rushed to my aid I began screaming, cursing and struggling so much that it took two of them to hold me down.

Once the scene was over I got a round of applause from the crew and later, when I met the film editor in the bar of the hotel, he said he'd just seen the day's rushes and it looked fantastic.

The experience of getting to know Stu and making the movie was incredible.

Reaction from the critics and public alike to the movie was fantastic. Soon after its release it gained five-star reviews, was given a special screening in the Houses of Parliament and was named among the top seven movies on Netflix. It also won several accolades, including a BAFTA for David Elliot for his portrayal of Mark Wright GC, who was killed at Kajaki.

Celebrity television presenter and columnist Jeremy Clarkson went as far as to say: 'Kajaki the True Story... may well be the best war film ever made'.

For me the greatest triumph of all was winning over the men from 3 Para and forging a lasting friendship with Stu

Pearson, who continues to selflessly help others, often acting as an ambassador for the army's medical rehabilitation
services and raising money for charity. He uses his experience to coach others on enduring physical hardship and the
importance of perseverance, determination and resilience to
overcome adversity. A hero in every sense.

31

Never judge the character by the script alone

Of all the roles I have been fortunate enough to play, both on stage and screen, the part of Ross the blacksmith in *Outlander* was probably one of the smallest. However, it has had the biggest impact on my life – by far!

Not only did I get to perform alongside some fantastic actors in a show that has been an extraordinary global hit but I also made many new friends, both in the virtual world of social media and real life.

When I was first approached about auditioning for a part in *Outlander* I was not aware of the colossal popularity it was enjoying in the USA, Canada, Australia and other countries. Indeed, very few people in Scotland were aware just how big a phenomenon it was at that time.

For various reasons the show was not broadcast in Scotland until six months after the independence referendum of 2014. It later transpired, from leaked emails, that then British Prime Minister David Cameron had met with Sony representatives to discuss delaying the show's screening for fear it would stir up Scottish patriotism and encourage a break-up of the United Kingdom.

Produced by Ronald D Moore of *Battlestar Galactica* fame and appearing on the Starz network in the US and Showcase in Canada, *Outlander* is based on a series of books by American author Diana Gabaldon, who also acts as an advisor for the show.

The story can best be described as a romantic, time-travel and historical adventure. It revolves around Claire Randall, played magnificently by Caitriona Balfe. She's a 1940s nurse who, while visiting an ancient stone circle in Scotland after the Second World War, unexpectedly falls through a time portal to Scotland of the 1740s, at the height of the Jacobite uprisings. Trapped in the past she meets and marries a handsome Highlander by the name of Jamie Fraser, played by Sam Heughan. The rest, as they say, is history – albeit one that has been embroidered with a fair bit of dramatic license and romantic fantasy.

In addition to becoming a global phenomenon, watched in over a dozen countries and voted Best Foreign TV Series/Serial award at the 23rd Shanghai TV Festival in 2017, *Outlander* has done wonders for the Scottish film industry. Through its success, hundreds, if not thousands, of people have found work, inspiration and success as actors, production crew and much more.

It has been a major boost to the local economy of Cumbernauld, North Lanarkshire where the studio is located, and helped raise Scotland's international profile with a new-found interest in the country's history, heritage, culture and products.

When I was first approached to audition for the show, I knew very little about how big a deal it was – and in retrospect I'm glad because it took a lot of pressure off.

My journey began when I got a call from my agent asking me to go to London and read for a role in a new television show called *Outlander*. I was told it was for a huge, 6ft5 hairy Highlander called Angus.

All the way from Glasgow to London on the train I kept thinking to myself that I was so wrong for the part. I was as far removed from the description of the character as it was possible to be. I'm not even six feet tall, I have never had a beard and nobody is ever going to confuse me with some muscle-bound warrior. However, I was determined to do my best.

I went into the audition determined to make an impression and I did, just not the right one. I had prepared a monologue but tried to put my own spin on it. It was just little things like changing a few words, such as maybe a yes to an aye and such like. It's pretty common for some actors to do this, after all you don't want to walk in and say the exact same things as the guy before you. It's a way of trying to stand out. Sometimes it works and sometimes it doesn't.

The casting agent was clearly determined to get me to say the lines exactly as they were written and made me redo the scene again and again, maybe as many as six times, before we were finished. Unsurprisingly I didn't get the part.

It was only much later, when I saw the first series of *Outlander* that I understood the character of Angus better. Although the script had called for a tall, well-built Highlander, the actor who got the part, Stephen Walters, didn't fit the bill any more than I had. But, Stephen had nailed it. He is a brilliant actor and I'm not surprised he got the role. His interpretation was much better than anything I would have done.

Although Stephen is quite small, certainly less than six feet tall, he had a smashing beard and, I found out later, had a secret trick up his sleeve to make his performance even more believable.

Stephen wears false teeth which he never usually takes out. But for his audition as Angus he did, so he looked much more like an authentic 18th-century character and got the part.

The lesson I took away from Stephen's story was never to judge the character by the script alone.

After my failed attempt at playing Angus I quickly forgot about the audition and went off to perform a play in Helsinki, Finland before taking the show to the Edinburgh Fringe Festival in the August.

It was just as we were finishing up in Edinburgh that year that I got another call from my agent about trying out again for a role in *Outlander*. This was the part of Ross, and although it was just three lines I was determined to make the most of it and not repeat my earlier mistakes.

I didn't have to go to London this time as the audition was in a little flat in Edinburgh, which was home to the casting director.

Determined to give it my best, I spent a lot of time researching the history and customs of the period in which the story is set. I worked out the politics of the whole scene and did an awful lot of prep for those three lines. By the time I finished I believed I had established for myself a believable back story for the character. And, most importantly, I was careful to learn the script exactly as it was written. I did not deviate at all this time. Thankfully, it must have worked.

A few days later Karen and I were enjoying a day out at Loch Lomond when I received a phone call from my agent informing me I had got the role. I was booked to be on set for four weeks of filming. I was delighted and immediately told Karen but her reaction was not what I expected.

Initially the smile on her face was as big as mine but within a split second it began to crumble and she burst into tears. In my excitement I hadn't realised the filming schedule clashed with our plans to go on holiday to Mexico. Karen had always wanted to visit the country and we had not had a proper vacation for at least two years. She had been going through a tough time at work and needed the break.

I rushed to give her a hug and promised I would phone the travel agent to rearrange the dates. We would just have to postpone. The agency was very kind, and for a fee of a few hundred pounds, they agreed to put back our date of departure to Mexico by six weeks.

By the time I arrived on set to begin filming the second series of *Outlander*, Sam Heughan, Caitriona Balfe, Tobias Menzies, Graham McTavish and the others had all been working together for the best part of two years or more.

Arriving for work on my first day reminded me of being the new kid in the park after we moved to Rutherglen. Just as it was then I wanted to get accepted by everybody else but didn't want to appear pushy or get in the way. I had to keep telling myself that all the stuff that was new to me was old hat to them.

I thought that as I only had three or four lines I would just sit out of the way and keep quiet. I wanted to watch and learn from all these great actors who had done such a fantastic job bringing series one to life.

On the day of my first read-through of the script I arrived early and tried to blend into the background.

As I sat down at the read-through table with the rest of the cast Sam Heughan tapped me on the shoulder and introduced himself. 'Hiya Scott, I'm Sam,' he said, as he stretched out his arm to shake my hand. I was so surprised that he, the big star of the show, would take time to find out who I was and go out of his way to make me feel welcome. I was soon to realise he wasn't the only one to be so friendly. Sam, Caitriona and the rest of the cast are very, very down to earth. They made a point of including everyone in the group and I was almost immediately invited on a night out with the cast.

The first day of filming felt so surreal. By this time I had watched the first season and been in awe at how they had brought the pages of Diana's books to life on the screen. Only when I walked on set did I realise how much of a major team effort is involved. There are hundreds of people involved in the production, each one of them at the top of their game working to make the show the best it can be. It's all very professional and everyone takes their job extremely seriously – although there were still quite a few lighter moments along the way.

On my first day filming with Sam, my character had to take off his top, lean over a barrel and get a public lashing in front of about 400 extras and all the crew.

It's a foam whip so it's not supposed to hurt, well that's the theory, but suffice to say that not every facial wince each time the whip made contact with my back was down to my fantastic acting ability. Thankfully the scene didn't take long to film and everything was great. Due to the fact that the set was all prepared and we still had some time, it was decided to film another scene, to be used later in the series, when Sam's character Jamie gets a lashing.

I was excited to watch because as it meant I could get to see what it all looked like from behind the camera. However, I admit to feeling a little put out when Sam walked onto the set and as he took his shirt off about 100 extras, mostly female, suddenly gasped, 'Ohhhhhhh'.

I remember thinking, 'Nobody did that when I took my shirt off. There were no gasps then!'

Jealousy aside, I learned some very valuable lessons during those first few days on location, not least how to plan your character's costume around the practicalities of filming.

Kajaki and most of my previous roles had been filmed either outside or inside, very rarely was there a combination of both. Picking a costume was therefore pretty straightforward. Unfortunately, being part of a production that involves being outside in all sorts of weather one day and in a studio packed with people and hot lights the next was something I hadn't thought much about.

When the make-up and costume teams were fitting me up they asked: 'Do you want gloves, do you want a hat?' I was like, 'Yeah, give me everything!'

While we were filming outside in the cold Scottish weather I felt really smug that I was nice and cosy while others, who had gone for less warm costumes, were shivering or rushing to put on big coats between takes.

But, come the next day, while filming in the studio in Cumbernauld I found myself suffering from the heat. I couldn't take anything off for continuity reasons so just had to sweat. Lesson learned!

When I was on set it seemed every day I was getting more to do as the character took on a life of his own. Each time I thought we had finished filming I would get invited back for the next week, and then again the following week.

The first time I was asked to stay on I almost blew it. I am a little embarrassed to admit now that when I was told they'd like to keep me on for another four weeks my initial reaction was, 'Oh no! How am I going tell the wife again that we're not going to Mexico?'

Fortunately, my agent made me see sense when I told him I wasn't sure about letting Karen down. He said bluntly, 'Scott, you're not going to Mexico.

You don't say no to *Outlander*. You're doing it.'

Initially I had been booked for four weeks and I ended up being on set for 12. It turned out to be among the most important three months of my life, and thankfully Karen didn't divorce me.

As my character evolved I got to work much more closely with other members of the cast. One scene involving my character, Ross, and Rupert, played by Grant O'Rourke called for us to get drunk and start singing the song 'Down Among the Dead Men'.

Grant had been on the show pretty much from the beginning so he was very experienced and very generous with his time and his advice. We spent quite a while before that scene exchanging ideas and suggestions of how we could play it. I owe a lot to Grant because he was absolutely fantastic to work alongside.

Other cast members were equally friendly and encouraging. One day I was sitting on the set, minding my own business, when a lassie came up to me and said Gary wanted to see me in his trailer. I couldn't understand why Gary Lewis, a big star who has appeared in a host of movies from *Gangs of New York* to *Billy Elliott*, would want to talk to me. I admit I was a little nervous, and wondered if I'd done anything wrong.

When I entered the trailer Gary asked me to read some lines with him, that's all. It was a very nice thing to do for somebody so new on the set and really helped to make me feel at ease and part of the team.

Caitriona Balfe was incredibly supportive in the limited scenes I had with her, especially the one in which my character's best friend dies from wounds inflicted at the Battle of Prestonpans.

On the day that was filmed I was dressed to the nines in my woollen Highlander garb, which had been great while we were outside but altogether less comfortable in the studio.

The script called for me to carry Gregor Firth, who played Kincaid, to Claire in a desperate effort to save his life. Unfortunately Gregor is a big lad and I couldn't carry him in my arms. The only way I could do it was to hoist him up over my shoulder in a fireman's lift. It took ten or 15 takes to get the shot and each time I had to run with Gregor over my shoulder. The sweat and exhaustion you see on my face in the final version is very real.

In the scene it is too late to save Kincaid and Claire says, 'There's nothing more I can do. I'm sorry.' Ross is devastated. He grabs Claire by the arm and parrot's the word 'Sorry?'

My job was to express the emotion of losing a best friend with all the hurt, regret, confusion and sadness that comes with that. It all had to be conveyed with facial expressions and a single word.

Cait was very kind and left the camera with me. As the lead actress on the show she could easily have done something that would have deflected attention from my character and stolen the scene but she didn't. I have always thought how that was both testament to her talent and her generosity as an actress. There are a lot of actors who would not have done that.

Sometimes the simplest things turn out to be the most difficult to do. There was one scene which involved me, Cait and Sam that took over 20 takes. The script called for my character Ross to carry a message to Jamie and Claire. I was to appear and say: 'Lord George requests your presence near the east dyke. You're to come at once.' Sam would turn, nod and say 'yes'. I then shut the door and that's the end of the scene.

While they were filming close-ups of Sam and Cait I had to feed them the line from off camera. I did it perfectly every time for about 20 takes and then they turned the camera around on me. As soon as the director said 'action' I fluffed the line and everybody started laughing. Thankfully I got it right the second time but that's the thing about filming, as soon as the camera is on you it's easy to lose focus or get distracted. Nobody wants to be the guy who has a reputation of forgetting his lines.

As is often the case while filming, especially when you are not one of the main characters, there is a lot of waiting around which can lead to a bit of boredom and, as a result, pranks.

Due to the way I had to carry Gregor in the Kincaid death scene some of the crew started referring me to as the fireman. It was something of a private joke between members of the cast and crew who had been on set the day we filmed that scene and I forgot that not everyone was in on it.

One day I was sitting in the green room with Romann Berrux, a talented French actor who played the young Fergus in seasons two and three of *Outlander*. He could only have been about 13 years old at the time.

While we were waiting to be called on to the set somebody called me Fireman. Romann wasn't in on the joke and thought I really had been a firefighter.

I asked if he wanted to hear one of my stories about life in the fire service and when he said yes I spun a fantastic tale of being called to a blaze in a high-rise tower block that was so tall we didn't have a ladder long enough.

Romann listened intently as I described a woman and baby trapped on a balcony too high for us to stage a rescue. As the flames got higher and the situation got perilous I claimed a giant of a man walked out from the crowd, with the biggest pair of hands I had ever seen.

I told Romann the man identified himself as Peter Čhek, the Arsenal goalkeeper who used to play for Chelsea. I doubt any soccer-loving British teenager would have fallen for my lies but Romann wasn't a football fan.

Warming to my story I said the man offered to catch the baby if the woman would drop the child from the balcony. I spun the tale out, claiming that at first we refused the offer but as things got more desperate, and the woman's cries for help got more frantic, I agreed to let the man help.

I remember Romann's eyes were as big as dinner plates as I described how the woman flung the baby from the balcony and Peter Čhek ran towards the building, his long arms outstretched as he dived and caught the child safely in his hands.

'For a moment everybody was ecstatic at such a miraculous rescue and a loud cheer went up from all the firefighters and watching bystanders,' I said.

'But, in that moment Peter forgot he wasn't playing a match, bounced the baby on the ground and kicked it into the air across the car park.'

When I looked at Romann his jaw had dropped and his mouth was wide open in shock as his brain processed what I had said. It took a couple of seconds for the penny to drop and he realised I'd been joking but by then tears of laughter were streaming down my cheeks. I'll never forget the look on his face.

Romann and I became good friends after that. He even attended some of my Highlander Flings as a guest in later years.

Being in a production like *Outlander* always looks fancier than it is. Yes, they often send a car for you in the mornings, people do your make-up and dress you, you sit in a trailer waiting for your scenes and then get escorted onto set and looked after tremendously. It all looks very glamorous but it's not.

The truth is all the special treatment is for the sake of the production, not the comfort of the cast. As an actor you are little more than a walking, talking prop. Most actors are so skint they send a car for us to make sure we show up on time and don't call in claiming to have missed the bus when we've slept in.

Other people dress us, style our hair and apply our make-up because we're not trusted to do it ourselves. We only get a trailer to sit in and get brought food and beverages so we don't wander off and get lost. In the film industry time really is money.

My part in *Outlander* finished towards the end of series two but unlike some others my character Ross didn't die at the battle of Culloden, even though he was initially supposed to.

The first episode of the third series starts with the aftermath of Culloden and all my friends who were in series two with me end up being killed, all that is except for Sam Heughan's character, Jamie Fraser.

In the initial draft of the script my character Ross was supposed to suffer the same fate as the other Jacobites, until Diana Gabaldon pointed out that earlier in the series Jamie had promised to see Ross safely home to Lallybroch. Jamie, being a man very much of his word, couldn't be seen to have failed in his promise so Ross wasn't killed off.

Unfortunately, although my character Ross survived, and there was for a brief time an online campaign among some *Outlander* fans to bring him back, my involvement in the show came to an end.

32

The Quintessential Scot(t)

Although my time on the television series was over, and I thought I was finished with *Outlander*, I quickly discovered the show, or at least some of the fans, weren't done with me.

After appearing on *Outlander* my social media following exploded beyond all expectations. At one time, before I actively started cutting it back, my X account had amassed a following of more than 750,000 people. At the time that was more than either Sam Heughan, the star of the show, or Diana Gabaldon, the writer of the books.

The only reason I can think of why so many followed me was because I always returned the compliment and engaged in online conversations with many. I've always thought that if people are kind enough to take an interest in what I do then it's only polite that I show some curiosity in them. I like engaging with people and *Outlander* fans in particular are fantastic. Some of them saw me as a connection with their favourite show, however tenuous, that they could reach out to.

A group of *Outlander* fans started a Kylander group on Facebook and even went as far as to design a tartan for it. Others began sending art works and handcrafted gifts, including knitted dolls of me, embroidered likenesses of my character and some stunning paintings.

One of the biggest compliments, at least in size, was a 4ft by 3ft multi-layered portrait of a kilted me created by artist Steven Hart. It was a remarkable piece of work, capturing almost all of my life in one image.

It took Steven four months to create 'The Quintessential Scot(t)', as he called it, using pencil, colour pencil, fine-line pens, graphic markers, and a touch of Kylander tartan material to create the kilt.

Each individual element, representing some aspect of my career, obsession with football, charity work and love for Scotland, was patiently created, cut out and pasted together to form a colourful and complex collage with an almost 3D effect.

Pretty quickly I didn't have room in my home to display the things people sent to me, even though I genuinely cherish every single item. It humbles me tremendously to think people I don't even know have put so much thought, effort, time and love into creating something for me. I ended up with so many items that my local library in Rutherglen offered to put on an exhibition.

Many of the *Outlander* fans who got in touch with me were fascinated by Scotland. They would often ask me questions about places, traditions and things that those of us who live in Scotland take for granted or seldom even think about. I always did my best to give an answer, but I admit some of the queries had me stumped or gave me something to think about.

It's sometimes difficult for native Scots to appreciate just how powerful the fascination for Scotland is among people abroad. Over the last couple of decades there's been a huge rise in interest in Scotland, particularly in the USA, among the diaspora who want to know more about their roots and family history.

Much of that curiosity has been fuelled, rightly or not, by Hollywood films such as *Braveheart*, *Rob Roy* and *Outlander*. They may not be the most historically accurate but they have awakened a giant interest in Scotland.

It is estimated that up to 50 million people worldwide claim to be descended from Scots, many of whom left Scotland because they were forced to during the Lowland and Highland Clearances. They didn't have any choice other than to try and build a new life in America, Australia, Canada, New Zealand or elsewhere. Stranded thousands of miles from family and friends many tried to keep alive some of their old traditions, and seized on new ones, that reminded them of home.

The yearning many had for their ancestral land was passed down in stories from one generation to the next over several hundred years and numerous places around the world were given Scottish names by homesick settlers.

Look at a gazetteer of the world and it's outstanding how many places have Scottish names. There are at least 15 places called Inverness, some 30 Aberdeens, 12 Edinburghs and five Dunedins – derived from the Gaelic name for Edinburgh. In the USA alone at least 21 communities bear the name Glasgow.

That great expat Scot Robert Louis Stevenson, author of *Kidnapped, Treasure Island* and *The Strange Case of Dr Jekyll and Mr Hyde,* who was born in Edinburgh and died in Samoa, understood the invisible bond very well. He wrote: 'The mark of a Scot of all classes is that he remembers and cherishes the memory of his forebears, good or bad; and there burns alive in him a sense of identity with the dead even to the twentieth generation.'

It is that sense of belonging which continues to encourage attendances at clan gatherings, Celtic fairs, festivals and Highland Games – the biggest of which is the annual Scottish Highland Gathering and Games in California. It attracts close to 50,000 spectators, more than double the attendance at the largest games in Scotland.

There are also millions of other people with no genetic or historical links to Scotland but who still feel an affinity with the place. The Gaels have a word for it. It is *cianalas*, pronounced key-an-a-lus, and it means a sense of longing or belonging to a place or time. It is a powerful force but one I didn't really appreciate until I launched my first Highlander Fling.

As the popularity of *Outlander* continued to grow and the number of my social media followers increased I began to get numerous requests to meet with fans when they came to Scotland. There were so many invitations to coffee that if I'd accepted them all I'd probably have ended up dead from a caffeine overdose.

My solution was to host an event to raise money for a good cause and invite anyone who wanted to meet me, and maybe some of my friends from the show.

Initially I thought I might get about a dozen people, if I was lucky, and we could take over the corner of a cafe or the back room of a pub for a chat and a laugh. But almost as soon as I floated the idea on social media the response was overwhelming.

Some people started planning holidays to Scotland to coincide with the date I suggested for everyone meeting up. Others booked flights and hotels. One woman, who couldn't afford a hotel on top of her travel expenses, ended up sleeping in my mum's spare room.

It was a crazy time. The enthusiasm was off the scale and with so many people willing to travel so far I knew I had to put on something a bit more memorable than coffee and cake. That's when the Highlander Fling was born.

More than 100 people, most of them from the US and Canada, turned up for the first one we did, in Bathgate.

It was an evening of extravagant Scottishness. We had neeps and tatties on the menu, a ceilidh band, Highland dancers, pipers and a few surprise guests, including Susan Boyle.

The event was a huge success, and not just for those who attended. Local hotels loved it because it brought people to Bathgate who would otherwise have probably gone elsewhere. The town kilt shop was over the moon because a lot of the *Outlander* fans were hiring outfits for the night. Even the local jeweller started making special souvenir pendants.

When everyone who had attended The Fling began talking about it and sharing photos on social media there was a big demand for it to become an annual event.

One thing I've learned from my time in entertainment is to always try to give the people what they want, but never rest on one's laurels. So that's exactly what I did.

The following year I moved The Fling to Linlithgow and spent months pulling it together. What started as a simple ceilidh became a five-hour showcase of Scottish talent. I hired dancers, musicians, pipe bands and invited some of my fellow cast members from *Outlander*, including Stephen Walters, who played Angus Mhor, as a surprise guest.

Each year The Fling would get bigger and better. People would come from Argentina, Sweden, America, England, Wales, Ireland and Germany, as well as some home-grown Scottish fans.

The surprise guest list would also get longer as I would invite some of the other cast members from *Outlander*, as well as faces from other films and shows I've done, such as *Kajaki*, *The Angels' Share* and *I'm No a Billy He's a Tim*. One year we even had actor Fraser Hines, whose role as the kilted Jamie McCrimmon in *Doctor Who* from 1966 to 1969, inspired Diana Gabaldon to write her series of *Outlander* books in the first place.

Whenever we had a Fling people would arrive in fantastic *Outlander*-style costumes they'd made themselves or dressed to impress in full Highland regalia. It was a truly amazing sight. It's that kind of audience participation that created such lively and fun evenings.

The Fling became an almost full-time job, especially when people started asking for similar events to be held in other countries. I couldn't do it all on my own so if anybody wanted to do their own thing they would have my blessing. I would be happy to show up and support it if I could.

Over the next couple of years Highlander Fling-style events started popping up around the world. There were some in Holland, France, Canada and several US locations, including New England and Florida.

Money raised by The Flings went to funding drama workshops for youngsters in this country and abroad. Teaching drama to children has always been a huge part of my career and it is very dear to my heart. Whether as a visiting lecturer at Edinburgh Acting School or delivering workshops to kids in France, Canada or the US it's been a way I can give back.

I wish somebody had given me more opportunities like that when I was a kid. I know from personal experience the impact my school drama teacher had on me. I didn't realise it then but those couple of hours a week in his class helped changed my life. Looking at what happened to some of my peers they may even have saved my life.

The Flings also began to play a useful role in supporting Scottish tourism. Each day, after the night before, I'd put on what I called the Hang Over Tour. I hired an open-top bus and took a party of up to 60 people to numerous tourist attractions. We visited sites such as Clydeside Distillery, the Transport Museum, Loch Lomond, Stirling Castle, Bannockburn and the Kelpies. One year we even went for a trip on the *Waverley* paddle steamer down the Clyde to Largs, just like millions of Glaswegians have done over the decades, and finished off with a visit to the Tennent's Brewery, home to the UK's largest beer attraction.

All in all I organised five annual Highland Flings until the global shutdown caused by the Covid pandemic put a bit of a damper on things. The world hasn't been the same since. I know I've changed. The enforced shutdown gave me time to think, to consider what is important in life and learn valuable lessons. For me it really was a big reset.

33
The pandemic

On 23 March 2020 the whirlwind that had been my life for at least the previous 16 years came to an abrupt halt. It was on that day that Prime Minister Boris Johnston announced the first UK lockdown and ordered everyone to stay at home because of the Covid pandemic sweeping the world.

To say it was a shock to the system is an understatement. For the first time in years I wasn't performing, producing, promoting or planning anything. It was as if somebody had flipped a switch and activated the emergency brake on my mind. Like a fully rigged sailing ship suddenly becalmed mid-ocean, everything came to a complete standstill. There was no metaphorical sound of crashing waves against my hull, blustering wind filling my sails propelling me forward at a high rate of knots, or squawking seabirds in the skies above coming at me in all directions. Just silence.

Like everyone else I initially found the idea something of a novelty and pottered around the house with Karen doing little domestic chores or working in the garden. But, as the days turned into weeks and then months I began to look back on my life and reassess my priorities. I was fast approaching 37 years old, a little young for a mid-life crisis perhaps but the compulsory downtime gave me time to think.

Acting has undoubtedly opened doors for me that I would never have expected when I was a cheeky little latch-key kid in Rutherglen. If anyone had told me then that I'd be on stage, appear in films and get to travel the world as the result of a television show I'd have thought they were crazy. And, if they had added that one day I'd get an invitation from Her Majesty Queen Elizabeth to attend a lavish garden party at one of her palaces I'd probably have laughed my head off.

Even now it feels unreal and hard to believe. I can just imagine what the young me, the one who wore second-hand football club jackets and hung around outside the chip shop at closing time for scraps, would have thought of my life in the run-up to the pandemic. He would have thought it an impossible dream, like something out of a movie.

Yet there I was in the summer of 2019, oblivious to the coming pandemic, having a ball. The Highlander Flings were growing in popularity, I was doing more charity events and working with a number of local theatres and community arts venues.

As if to highlight just how well everything seemed to be going, out of the blue one day, I received an invitation in the post to attend a Royal Garden Party. Apparently someone had put my name forward in recognition of various charity works I'd been involved with. It was definitely a complete surprise but, never one to squander a chance to dress up in a kilt and see my wife Karen put on her posh frock and hat, I was happy to accept.

The Palace of Holyrood House, situated at the end of the Royal Mile in Edinburgh, is the monarch's official residence in Scotland. It is open to visitors throughout the year and is full of history, having been associated with some of Scotland's most famous figures such as Mary, Queen of Scots and Bonnie Prince Charlie.

Just walking in their footsteps is exciting. On the day of the party my dad picked us up in his taxi, which had been wrapped in an advertisement for the Highlander Fling, and dropped us off outside the palace. We made sure to be nice and early as security was very tight. Everyone on the guest list had to bring at least two forms of photo identification and all bags were searched as we passed through the gates under the watchful eye of armed guards on the roof of the building.

There were thousands of people, all of them invited in recognition of things they had done to help their communities in some way or another. It was a very humbling experience to meet such great folk from all walks of life, each of them with a great story to tell about working for charities, developing arts projects, or serving in the military.

The best part of the day for me was seeing the smile on Karen's face. She looked amazing and it was great to see her enjoying it. She's had to put up with quite a lot over the years, staying up late waiting for me to get home from a theatre play or my disappearing for weeks on end to make a movie.

When I saw her standing in the sunshine, her eyes sparkling, stray strands of her long blonde hair fluttering in the slight breeze, I was struck just how happy she looked at that moment. If I hadn't already been in love with her I think I would have fallen head over heels on the spot. I remember wondering if life for us could ever get any better. As it turned out, it could and would. Just not quite in a way I ever considered at that time.

In the months before anyone had any idea of what was coming, with regard to Covid and the damage lockdown would do to the arts, my diary was filling up nicely. I was planning another Highlander Fling in Glasgow, plus at least two more in the USA. I was working with a couple of different theatre schools, teaching workshops to youngsters. I was lined up to play at the Edinburgh Fringe Festival and scheduled to start filming a movie in London. There were also some theatre projects on the horizon. Life was very busy and for me that meant it was good.

The pandemic took care of all of that. As an actor, like any freelance or self-employed person, if you don't have work you don't get paid. In keeping with the plight of many thousands of other people, I saw my income and earning potential fall to zero overnight.

However, being forced to take a break made me realise I had built a never-ending hamster wheel for myself. For years I had been going from one project to the next, never turning down a job or an opportunity for fear there might never be another. Now I had time to draw breath. The whole show business industry had come to an almost complete stop. There was no longer any worry about missing out on anything because nothing was happening.

To make ends meet I took a job with a local charity supporting folk that couldn't get out of their own house or look after themselves. I would do grocery shopping for them and help in their homes. It was just a few days a week but I found I really enjoyed being a care worker.

One job especially changed me in ways I never thought possible. I was tasked with helping to look after a young teenage boy, who I'll call Adam out of respect for him and his family's privacy.

Adam is a lovely young man but he is autistic and therefore his behaviour can be challenging at times. I was asked to help look after him two days a week to give his mother some respite. Getting to know Adam was one of the best experiences I have ever had. It changed my life and, I'd like to think, his.

My days with Adam consisted of me heading up to his house in the morning to pick him up and then we'd go out for the day. His mother wanted him to experience new things and to get out of the house for a short time. Adam and I would go walking, hill climbing or cycling. We would go to parks, cycle by the river or visit places I would probably never have gone on my own.

Over time I found myself planning our outings on my days off, and spending more than my allotted time with Adam because I genuinely enjoyed his company. I didn't mind going over and above my contracted work hours.

There are some jobs that even when you put everything you have into them it doesn't work out. It never feels worthwhile or that you are achieving anything. There was never a time working with Adam that I thought I was wasting my energy. I could see how much he enjoyed our activities. I felt I was helping to change somebody's life. It was certainly changing mine.

Karen noticed it too. One day she mentioned I appeared more excited about stuff I was doing with Adam, and other people I helped look after, than I was with some of the movies and theatre shows I'd done. She was right.

Being able to get out of the house and see people made the tribulations of the pandemic more tolerable for me in some ways. For Karen that wasn't so easy. I think lockdown was probably much harder on her. We are both very sociable people and not being able to visit friends and be with family was very difficult. Home alone while I was working meant Karen had time to think about our life.

Karen has always wanted to have children. I truly believe she was born to be a mother and has all the qualities to be a very good parent. She came from a loving, stable home and naturally wanted to pass that on to children of her own. I, on the other hand, was a bit more resistant based on my experiences. Of course I wanted kids too, but there was always another show or project to get out of the way first.

Karen and I were together 13 years before marrying, and that delay was down to me. I was worried marriage might spoil what we had; it certainly did with my parents, or at least that's what I believed and feared for a long time. I was always finding excuses in my own head for putting off starting a family. I thought I needed to wait for a perfect time and that I would recognise that moment when I saw it.

However, as I realise in retrospect, Robert Burns was uncannily correct when he wrote his poem 'To a Mouse' and said, 'The best-laid schemes o' Mice an' Men / Gang aft agley / An' lea'e us nought but grief an' pain, / For promis'd joy!' In other words, 'make plans and give God a laugh'.

Earlier in our relationship I thought I'd wait until we were married and had a house before having a family. But, then I didn't want to get married until I felt financially secure. Only, when I did have money I used it for other things, like paying off my mum's mortgage and her other debts, or decorating her flat.

Looking back I guess I thought there was always plenty of time. Delaying marriage and family for a few more years surely couldn't hurt?

One day Karen turned to me and said, 'Sometimes I think if you hadn't given your mum all that money we would have had kids by now.'

That was very hard for me to hear, even though I admit the thought had crossed my mind several times.

The last thing in the world I would ever want to do is to let Karen down but her saying that out loud made me seriously consider that maybe I had.

Everyone has a story in their head of their life. What most of us forget is that, like every other tale, there is always an alternative interpretation. In one version of my story, the one where I help my mum, I'm a hero. But in the substitute narrative, in which I fail to appreciate Karen's needs, I am the villain.

Suddenly, I could imagine Karen's parents sitting in their house watching me on television or reading about me in a magazine and saying to themselves, 'That's great, Scott but our daughter is desperate for a family and you've wasted that opportunity for her.'

After years of thinking time was on my side and waiting for the perfect moment to have a family I began to fear I'd left it too late.

In the run-up to the pandemic Karen and I had embarked on a series of in vitro fertilisation (IVF) treatments in an attempt to have a baby. The whole process and numerous side effects of the medications were very demanding on Karen, both physically and emotionally.

We had been trying for three years to have a baby naturally without any luck. Even though doctors assured us there was no diagnosed reason why we had been unable to conceive, we realised time was against us so decided to try IVF.

In one of my favourite photographs taken at the Queen's Garden Party, Karen had just finished her first cycle of IVF treatment. Her body had started to prepare itself for being pregnant.

The first round seemed to go alright, although Karen suffered from hyper-stimulation and increased blood pressure. A total of 16 eggs were fertilised, 11 took after fertilisation and we were really hopeful. However, after just five days only three eggs were left. Karen took a pregnancy test two weeks later and found it was negative.

We tried a second time, which involved Karen having to take a different set of drugs. Unfortunately the side effects of these were worse than the first lot. They made her much more emotional and Karen found it tougher to deal with than the first attempt. There were other ramifications too. Karen suddenly developed a long-term cough which forced her to take time off work and at least two courses of antibiotics before doctors eventually diagnosed it as Asthma. She also developed an allergy to cat and dog hair she'd never suffered from before.

Again the IVF didn't work and with the toll it took on her physical health Karen understandably felt disappointed and that it had been a lot to endure for nothing.

However, we knew the odds were against us. Neither of us had gone into the process blindly. Karen had a friend who fell pregnant after three rounds of IVF. Her cousin had to undergo ten rounds before she got pregnant. We knew things didn't always work out but that didn't stop the feelings of disappointment.

Undeterred, Karen worked even harder on her fitness and diet as we prepared to go again. We really thought this third time was going to be a charm.

She had been taking all the medications needed in preparation for the egg transfer and had even being undergoing a course of acupuncture at a clinic where there was a wall plastered in photos of miracle babies.

Then, two days before she was to undergo the egg transfer the hospital rang to say due to the pandemic all treatment was being stopped as the doctors were needed elsewhere.

It was an extremely stressful time for the both of us, especially when appointments had to be delayed or cancelled. Due to the impact the processes were taking on Karen's health, and the uncertainty surrounding what was happening with Covid, we decided to stop the IVF and re-evaluate our options.

In many ways our failure to conceive was made even harder for Karen than it was for me. Due to the restrictions on movement imposed by the pandemic, she couldn't just go and be with her mum, brother and his kids. She was left at home alone with her thoughts while I was out working as a carer.

As the months of lockdown progressed I began working in other areas of the welfare sector, particularly with children in residential care. I spent a couple of nights a week doing support shifts and I saw first-hand kids in need of a family.

It was around then I saw a notice appealing for people to volunteer as foster parents. There are thousands of children in Scotland and across the UK in care yet the number of people willing to foster, or being approved for the role, is falling.

When I thought how much Karen and I could offer I took the advertisement home and suggested the idea. It wouldn't be easy, we knew that. But there were children out there who needed support. We have a nice house, two spare bedrooms, the time and willingness to help. We decided to apply.

34
Fostering a new life

Having decided to explore the possibility of becoming foster parents, Karen and I began researching the qualities and personalities required for the role. After several months of study and a lot of deep discussions, we put in an application.

The first thing we had to do was wait. The authorities won't consider anyone undergoing IVF for at least 12 months after all treatment has stopped. I suppose it's in case those applying are doing so out of some kind of knee-jerk reaction to not being pregnant. They also want to know that prospective carers have really thought about what they are doing and understand the responsibilities and commitments involved.

When the wait was over we had to undergo a variety of stringent background checks, interviews, counselling sessions and training courses. Both Karen and I were interviewed together and separately on several occasions as part of a deep dive into our past experiences and their impact on our lives now.

No topic was off the agenda. They wanted to know, and see, how we would view or deal with issues of aggression, sexism, racism, homophobia, sectarianism, gender identities, eating disorders, disabilities, trauma, mental illness, emotional issues and a host of other things most parents never consider they might have to deal with or encounter when they have children naturally.

One of the most surprising things about being a foster carer is the amount of time it takes to do the training and all the background checks, including getting references from all manner of people, ranging from childhood friends and family to doctors and social workers.

They say it takes a village to raise a child and the authorities overseeing the foster system want to know that prospective carers have a wide support network of their own. We are fortunate in having Karen's mum and dad, as well as her brother and his family, just streets away. We also have a lot of close friends, people we have known for years, who we can rely on for help whenever we might need it.

As foster parents you are not just welcoming children into your home and own life but, by extension, the lives of all your family and friends.

We made a decision early on in the process that my parents would not be as actively involved as Karen's family. In part this was due to the location of where they live, but also it was about the relationship that Karen and I have with my mother and father.

We hadn't fallen out or anything. It was just that the way in which we live our lives, and the hopes we had of being a positive influence on any child placed with us, was different from the way my mum and brother lived. As for my dad, I hadn't seen him for over 20 years and only fairly recently had started to rebuild a relationship.

My mum didn't like the idea of me working with Adam as a carer and she wasn't as supportive of us trying IVF or applying to be foster parents as Karen's folks were. I am not exactly sure why.

However, right or wrong, I have drawn on my experiences and how they continue to impact my life in a way that I've set a new benchmark of how I want to live. I don't want drama, alcohol, drugs or anything negative around me.

When we started the fostering process we were made aware that some of the children we might be asked to look after come from families where there has been a history of domestic violence, alcoholism or such like.

To have a positive effect on some of these children's lives I believe the best thing I can do is to try and help them break the negative cycle of substance abuse, violence, negativity or low self-esteem which they might have been exposed to.

Karen and I don't allow alcohol in our home. It's just not something we need to enjoy ourselves or relax. When I was growing up I never smoked and I never drank despite seeing it all around me at home. I was 16 before I had my first alcoholic drink and among my peers at the time that was considered old.

Sadly, statistics for alcohol and drug use among children in Glasgow are staggering. Reports suggest that girls aged 13 to 15 are more likely to drink than boys, but when the lads do start they are more likely to get drunk more often. In places like Easterhouse, children as young as eight or nine have been diagnosed with drinking problems.

Other studies claim almost a quarter of 15-year-olds in Glasgow have tried drugs. That's higher than the national average across Scotland.

I was lucky as a youngster because I was confident enough without drink. I saw the upset and damage it had caused within my own family and I didn't like it. Something I have always tried to pass on to the kids in my acting classes is that if somebody tries to goad you into doing something you're not comfortable with then it is cool to say no.

They say the definition of insanity is doing the same thing over and over again in expectation of a different result. Sadly, a lot of people don't learn from their mistakes. On the other hand, it is true that 'a wise man learns from his mistakes but a wiser man learns from the mistakes of others'.

There are those who might argue that our fate is sealed by our genes but I don't subscribe to that. While I understand the power of genetics I firmly believe from my own observations and experience that outside influences can help dictate the path we take in life.

As a child I loved going to my pal's house where there was always food in the fridge, perfumed scented polish filled the air, they sat down together to eat and every Friday was family takeaway night. It was such a far cry from my home and violent arguments most weekends fuelled by carry-outs of booze rather than food, and a permanent smell of stale tobacco smoke.

When Karen met my dad for the first time she was struck by how much Craig was like him in the way he talked and mannerisms. However, she concluded I was more like my dad in the way he thought.

When he met my mum he saw what her home life was like. It was so different from his. In my mum's family they sat and talked to each other instead of getting drunk and fighting. It was a home where his clothes were washed and dinner was on the table when he got home from work. I think he thought if my mum was going to turn out like her mother, Sadie, he would have it made.

Unfortunately my mum wasn't like that. She wanted to rebel against the order he was looking for. As a result their relationship became volatile and toxic. It wasn't until my dad met Margaret, my step-mum, that he stopped drinking and learned to turn his life around to get something of what he had always been looking. Margaret is his Karen.

Genetics, or nature, is important but it doesn't have to define who we are. I learned a lot from the likes of Wayne Dyer about the power of nurture. He inspired me to change my behaviour and outlook on life.

For many people many of the insights he preaches are second nature but they weren't for me. My parents were absent for a lot of my childhood so I didn't have anyone to explain to me the little life hacks others take for granted. I had to make a lot of it up as I went along, which resulted in quite a few mistakes on the way.

However, it's worth saying that my situation, just like millions of other kids around the world, wasn't solely down to poverty. My parents may not have been around for various reasons but there are rich kids too who don't get taught these lessons. Their parents are off leading lives of their own and think that throwing cash at a problem is preparation enough for a good life. Money isn't everything, sometimes what kids need more than anything is time, attention and guidance.

Shortly after being approved to become foster parents, I got the chance to put my beliefs and theories into action when Karen and I were asked to care for an 11-year-old boy and his sister, aged ten.

They had been living with three siblings and their mother in circumstances similar to those I had experienced, which is partly why I think we were asked to help.

Initially it felt strange but within a week they were loving their new home with us. For the first time in their lives they each had a bedroom to themselves.

As the weeks and months passed they got to know us and we them. We went on outings to the cinema, which neither had ever done before. We took walks in the park, fed the ducks, went cycling and helped them with their school homework.

Every fortnight we would take them to spend time with their three siblings, who were being fostered by another family, and even a couple of caravan holidays which was an all-new experience for them.

I even had them help deliver leaflets for my show *Billy & Tim* at 10p per door. It was the first time they had ever had money of their own and loved it.

Within a very short space of time it felt as though we were a family of four. Karen and I love them to bits and as far as we are concerned they have a home with us for life.

It has been an amazing experience for us watching the kids learn simple skills to avoid conflict, to be less demanding or self-centred and to think of others.

When they first came to us there was a lot of me, myself and I in their demands; now it's you, we and us. I can totally understand where they were coming from. They lived in a home where it was every person for themselves. They had to battle each other for attention, snacks, toys or whatever. I can identify with those behaviours in many ways because I was like that and I saw it in many of the families my friends came from.

I've also taught them little things that help people to warm to you, such as never using the 'Naked Thank You'. It may sound obvious but when you get off the bus instead of just saying 'thanks' to the driver in the same way and tone as everyone else, elaborate a little. If you say something like 'Thanks for looking after us', or 'Thanks for getting us here safely', it's more likely to be heard and appreciated. It's called value added context and it can transform how people engage with you.

I remember when I went to the library to look for my first play to put on. I came across a book on body language in the psychology section and it fascinated me. It gave me my first real education on how to interact with people in different situations.

I came from a boisterous street and football background where it was not only acceptable to be rude or abrasive with others it was considered banter and expected. If you were good at taking the mickey out of somebody among the football crowd you could be viewed as an absolute legend, one of the boys. Do that in the theatre world and there's a good chance you'll end up upsetting people and being labelled a prat, or worse.

Quite early on in our relationship I took the kids to the library and got them library cards. I explained that it was more than just proof of identification, it was a symbol of trust. They were being trusted to borrow a book, look after it and return it. Somebody was putting faith in them. Nobody did that for me when I was a kid and it was the first time anyone had done that for them.

Overtime the kids have matured and become more comfortable in different situations. I first realised some of the tips I was passing on were taking hold when we all went to a big, important meeting with their case workers. At the end of the proceedings the chairperson went round everyone in the room and asked if they had anything to add. When they got to the kids the wee man said, 'No, but thanks for asking.' It may seem like a tiny thing to most people but it was a big change for this kid. I don't mind admitting my heart felt fit to burst with pride.

When I was in foster care as a wee boy, albeit for a very short time, I hated it and the people that took me away from my mum. Now, I understand why and how important fostering is. I've now become part of the support network that benefited me. It is undoubtedly one of the best things I have ever done. There is nothing more precious than being trusted enough to look after two other people.

When I look back at my childhood I would never have thought I would be fostering kids as an adult. Mind you, I never imagined that one day I would be swapping parenting tips with Hollywood icon Harrison Ford either.

35

Whit's fur ye'll no go by ye

There's a saying in Scotland that 'whit's fur ye'll no go by ye' and experience has shown me there's a lot of truth to it, especially when I consider how close I came to missing out on a dream experience.

It might not have been a part in the *Indiana Jones* or *Star Wars* movie franchises, but getting to work alongside Hollywood icon Harrison Ford felt like a blockbuster opportunity for me. And to think I almost said no.

Television adverts have never really been my thing. Over the years I've been asked to audition for a few but it's not something I'm passionate about. I like storytelling, and that usually means a stage play, movie or television show.

So, when I was asked to try out for a project promoting whisky, being filmed in the Highlands of Scotland, my first instinct was to say no. I was already juggling my responsibilities as a foster parent, a full-time job and rehearsals for a new play. The prospect of having to take a couple of days out of my already busy week to drive hundreds of miles for what I thought would be a tiny background part in a 30-second commercial didn't immediately appeal.

However, I'd just signed with a new agent and didn't want to say no to one of the first things they offered me. Reluctantly I agreed to take on the part, which I was told was playing a warehouse worker. That's all I knew when I set off from Glasgow one Tuesday afternoon, following a long shift, to drive more than 200 miles from Glasgow to Tain, near Inverness.

Due to contractual reasons the company behind the product being promoted won't allow me to divulge anything about the making of the advert, which has been turned into a series of commercials.

However, there was a lot of international publicity surrounding the project when it was announced that Glenmorangie Highland single malt Scotch whisky had launched 'a new global campaign starring cinematic icon, Harrison Ford'.

The official press release said: 'Legendary for his count-less iconic movie roles, the Hollywood actor brings his trade-mark wry humour to the fore in a series of episodic films directed by actor and film-maker Joel Edgerton.

'Once Upon a Time in Scotland takes us behind-the-scenes as Harrison Ford journeys to Glenmorangie's High-land home, to discover the skill and craftsmanship that goes into making each bottle of its complex and elegant whisky. It sees the actor enjoy the authentic Scottish experience – from getting to grips with the nuances of Scottish pronunci-ation and kilt etiquette, to bonding with locals over a dram of single malt – all shot in an unconventional, deliberately 'off-script' style.

'Filmed in the picturesque north-east Highlands of Scot-land, the campaign captures the natural beauty of the local area: from the historic distillery in Tain where Glenmo-rangie has been created for over 180 years, to the storied 19th century Ardross Castle, and the dramatic landscapes surrounding Loch Glass. Appearing alongside Ford are the real Glenmorangie distillery team – who embraced their first experience of acting under the guidance of a global cine-matic legend.'

The first I knew about Harrison Ford being involved was when he arrived on set. Just meeting the guy was a pleasure so you can imagine my surprise, and obvious delight, when I was told I'd have a one-to-one scene with the Hollywood icon.

'Once Upon a Time in Scotland' was rolled out globally from 28 January 2025 spanning online video, connected TV, out-of-home formats, experiential, PR and social media.

The six full-length episodes, including the two in which I featured, and an array of behind-the-scenes content can be seen on glenmorangie.com.

36

Sometimes the call of the past is too strong

They say you should never go back but sometimes the call of the past is too strong. Provided we have learned from our mistakes, and are sensible enough to see a possible new direction, then perhaps there can be an exception that proves the rule. At least I hope so.

In the run-up to the 20th anniversary of the year I first produced *Singin' I'm no a Billy He's a Tim* I received a phone call out of the blue from Des Dillon, the writer of the play. We'd met a few times over recent years and our relationship could probably be best described as cordial but distant. Even now I have occasional flashbacks to the night he told me he was taking back control of the production. That moment haunts me and still has the power to quicken my pulse as a shiver of regret runs down my spine.

However, hindsight is a wonderful thing. I realise that although losing the play was without doubt one of the worst times in my life, that moment was instrumental in helping to shape the person I am now. It forced me out of my comfort zone and propelled my career in a variety of different directions I might otherwise never have explored.

I fully understand that Des's actions back then were not in any way personal or a reflection on my abilities. It was purely and simply a business decision, but it still hurt.

In the years since losing the show I have seen posters for different productions at various venues but I could never bring myself to go see any of them. I guess it was like losing a great love. *Billy & Tim* was my 'one that got away' and I didn't like seeing it in the arms of someone else. The pain may have eased over time but the wound never fully healed. Thoughts of 'what if', 'maybe I could have' and 'if only' continued to lurk in the dark recesses of my mind to jump out and surprise me when I least expected.

Billy & Tim was more than a show to me. Five years of living and breathing the play, planning and plotting how to make it better and more popular, walking probably thousands of miles posting promotional flyers through doors to attract new audiences, all had a big impact on my life. It was my first success, it won me a theatrical award and it put more money in my bank account than I had ever dreamed of. Overnight it was gone and it was a bitter pill to swallow.

So when, in September 2023, Des unexpectedly contacted me asking if I'd be interested in taking on the play again, I was surprised to say the least.

It felt a little surreal, like having a romantic partner from the distant past suddenly get in touch. Mixed emotions of excitement, apprehension, suspicion and curiosity whirled around my mind. Years after ruthlessly and unceremoniously being dumped and made to watch from the sidelines as other guys had their fun, my first love now suddenly wanted to rekindle our relationship.

It took a minute for the words coming out of Des's mouth to connect with my brain, but when they did I was left almost speechless. For what seemed like several minutes, but in reality was only a second or two, I paused. It was as if inside my head there were two Scotts vying to be heard. The old me, the brash boy from the streets of Rutherglen, was thinking along the lines of 'tell him to get tae…', 'not bloody likely', 'once bitten twice shy', 'my heid disnae button up the back ye ken', and 'how dare you ask me that after what happened'.

Alternatively, the older, and hopefully wiser, me was more considerate. I managed to stifle my initial knee-jerk reaction and took time to reflect. 'I'll have to think about it and speak to Karen,' I calmly replied.

As we'd had our lives turned upside down once before I wasn't sure how Karen would react to the idea. I discussed the matter with her and a couple of friends and, almost unanimously, their initial response was to walk away and keep moving on. But, one never forgets their first love. I could see some sense in doing the play again. I knew it inside out. I had a good idea of how to update it and attract new audiences. Also, I had unfinished business with this play.

Back in the day I had planned to take *Billy & Tim* to London's West End, but that had been scuppered because Des wouldn't accept a lower share of royalties. I had wanted to take the show to New York, perhaps as part of the annual Tartan Week celebrations. I also thought, with a little refinement, it could appeal to expat Scots and the diaspora living in Australia, Canada, New Zealand and elsewhere. They were dreams I never got to fulfil. Could this be a second chance?

After much thought and debate, Karen's view was that it was up to me, but she urged me to be very careful. She had seen up close how losing the show had affected me last time. The opinions of my friends were similar. If I was going to do it there must be no more handshake deals. They advised me to get it all in writing, and make sure everything was legally watertight.

I called Des back and arranged to meet for a chat. It turned into a long discussion as I outlined the terms I would need before taking back *Billy & Tim*. To my surprise there was no argument. We cleared the air and agreed to move on.

The first thing I did the next day was to go and talk to a lawyer. I got a clear contract drawn up for both of us to sign. Now, after 20 years, I felt as if at last I had my baby back, only this time it was on my terms.

Just as I did when I first read the play all those years before, I reached out to my former college friends and got the old band back together. With Colin Little playing Tim, James Miller as Harry the turnkey, and me as Billy, I knew we could recapture those glory days of the past.

We had toured together for five years, so we know each other's performances inside and out. If Colin says a certain line it's ingrained in me what to reply. We've done the show so many times it's a blessing to be on that stage together. We went through all the highs and the lows of the original production as a team and we have a genuine love for each other.

However, I realised much has changed in the last 20 years, not least the fact that the three of us are no longer young tearaways but middle-aged men. When we started touring *Billy & Tim* midway through the 2000s, YouTube had just been launched and Facebook was less than a year old. There was no TikTok, X, Netflix downloads or other similar streaming services. There is now a generation of people who weren't even born when we started. How could they relate to three guys who look more like their dads than their mates? There would have to be compromises.

Adapting *Billy & Tim* for new audience demographics seemed like a no-brainer but I didn't want to alienate people of our own age and even older. The solution turned out to be both simple and complicated. The idea was easy but implementing it more difficult. I would produce several adaptations of the play for different audiences. It had the additional benefit of creating work for more young actors, and after all that is exactly why I set up my NLP theatre company in the first place.

Colin, James and I would continue playing our parts, albeit as older characters that people around our age would recognise. Almost everyone knows somebody whose attitudes are stuck in the past and never matured in line with their bodies.

Then, running alongside the original play would be another interpretation using younger actors. Their performances would better relate to the new generation.

Within months we had two adaptations of the play out on tour appealing to different age groups. The idea worked so well I decided to go even further with an all-female cast performing an alternative version called *Singin' I'm No a Billie, She's a Tim*.

Recent years have seen a surge in the number of women both playing and watching football. Various reports and surveys have suggested that up to a third of fans following premier league football are female so it seemed like a natural progression.

When we put together the first all-female shows at the Edinburgh Fringe Festival the response was amazing. The chemistry between the three actors, Jade McDonald playing Tim, Dionne Frati as Billie, and Rachel Ogilvy as Harriet the jailer, was explosive. Their energy was infectious, their timing spot on and slapstick comedy hilarious. One minute the audience was silently captivated by their poignant performances and the next roaring with laughter.

Marketing the show was also a lot of fun. At the Fringe in 2024 performers from around 60 countries put on almost 3,750 shows across more than 260 venues. All of them were trying to capture public attention and a share of the 2.6 million tickets sold.

To get noticed in such a competitive market you have to be really creative. So, while walking the streets of Edinburgh promoting *Billy & Tim*, the cast and supporters all wore specially designed 'half and half' football tops. I had these custom-made to represent both the Rangers blue and Celtic green hoops. The strips were a great conversation starter and we had lots of people taking selfies with us, including several of the city's police officers and world-famous actor Richard E Grant. He was visiting the Fringe at the time and when he spotted the girls wearing their distinctive football jerseys he stopped for a chat.

During the four-week run at the festival the show garnered three five-star reviews, which was incredible. Diana Gabaldon, author of *Outlander*, even took to social media to congratulate the girls and praise their achievement.

After giving young men and women their own versions of the play it was time to give older folk, like me, their turn, albeit with a little twist. I managed to talk two retired foot-ball stars, Charlie Miller of Rangers, and Simon Donnelly of Celtic into making their theatrical debuts with cameo-style performances.

These men are Old Firm legends. Charlie worked his way up through the Rangers youth system and played a key role in the club's 1990s nine-in-a-row Scottish League victories.

Simon was equally revered by Celtic fans for his skill on the pitch. He spent seven years at the club, making more than 140 league appearances and scoring 30 goals.

I'm lucky to have known both men for years. We grew up in the same area. Simon and I went to the same school, Stonelaw High, though he was a few years above me.

Charlie was also a familiar face around the neighbour-hood. When I was a wee boy we used to play in Springhall and if Charlie was passing he would sometimes jump over the fence and kick the ball about with us.

When I approached them to join the show they jumped at the chance. Their addition to the cast helped add a whole new layer of excitement for the audience, especially when they took part in a question-and-answer session at the end of the play.

The promotional tagline was easy. 'What could be worse for a Celtic legend and a Rangers legend than being locked up in a police cell together on the day of the Old Firm match? For Simon Donnelly and Charlie Miller, there is one thing worse, being banged up with fervent Old Firm supporters Billy and Tim!'

Billed as 'Singin' I'm No a Billy He's a Tim with the Old Firm Legends' it has been a tremendous success. It has sold out everywhere it has played and done a lot to help bring both sides closer together.

Billy & Tim is first and foremost entertainment. It is not supposed to be an educational platform, but no doubt some audiences do learn a lesson from it. I have spoken to lots of people who have seen it and admitted it made them uncomfortable. It made them think twice about singing particular songs next time they're at Rangers' home stadium of Ibrox or Celtic's Parkhead.

Although we have updated the script to include mentions of hate crime legislation, the conflict in Gaza, war in Ukraine and other divisions in the world, the message ultimately remains the same. There is no place in a civilised world for prejudice and division.

I am tremendously proud that after 20 years *Billy & Tim* is still one of the most successful touring Scottish theatre shows of the modern era.

A brand-new re-write of the original script and a variety of special performances tailored to appeal to different audiences has meant there is still plenty of mileage left in the show. It continues to entertain audiences of all ages, classes, creeds and genders. It remains an important vehicle in the struggle against bigotry and division wherever it raises its ugly head.

37

You're no Billy Connolly

When I told my older brother Craig I was writing this book he laughed and said, 'That's for the likes of Billy Connolly and you're no Billy Connolly.'

He is right of course. I am not Billy Connolly, nor have I achieved anything close to the level of success, fame and money he has. I am just an ordinary, working-class boy from the back streets of Rutherglen.

My story is no different from countless other youngsters. Statistics show almost 24 percent of children in Scotland live in relative poverty.

It is sad to think that despite all the technological advances and wealth of the country, the childhood of almost a quarter of a million Scottish kids in the 21st century is the same, if not worse, than that I experienced in the 20th century.

'*Plus ça change, plus c'est la même chose*,' as the French say. The more things change, the more they stay the same.

Reflecting on my formative years I could easily have fallen into a life of crime, violence, alcohol, drugs and despair. Why didn't I?

Italian novelist and poet Cesare Pavese once said: 'We do not remember days, we remember moments.' It is how we emotionally interpret and react to those moments in hindsight that shapes us.

Yes, I have flashbacks of seeing my mother being battered by her lover, trembling in fear at the sound of his key in the lock. I remember the heartbreak at not seeing my father, grieving over old school friends killed in tragic circumstances and the ever-present fear of violence in the street.

But I also have memories of the football coaches who taught me to play and gave me second-hand clothes so I could fit in with the other boys. The drama teacher who put trust in me, the college lecturers who gave me a chance to act, Karen's parents who encouraged me back to college. Wayne Dyer's words to live and let live.

I could have chosen to follow the negative path and repeat the cycle but instead I chose to dwell on the positive moments. I believe everything that has happened to me was meant, so that I could learn. I am where I am, and the man that I am because of, and not in spite of, the experiences I have had. It is true, in many ways, that what doesn't kill you will make you stronger.

I've always tried to give something back by paying it forward. It is a philosophy that has served me well. When I sponsored a youth football team it was because somebody did it for me when I was a wee boy playing for a team. I could never have been able to afford to buy a football shirt myself back then.

It's the same with a lot of the acting workshops I do for youngsters. I do it because somebody took the time to do it for me. I firmly believe that if I can return the favour, even after all these years, then I should.

If it hadn't been for the pandemic I wouldn't have been looking for work outside the theatre and the arts. I would never have had to take a job in the care system. I would never have had the privilege of meeting Adam or some of the other people I had the honour of helping.

I think if Karen and I had kids of our own we probably wouldn't have gone down the fostering route and that has turned out to be one of the best, most rewarding experiences of our lives.

I may not be a millionaire with piles of cash in the bank or a hoard of material things but I do have riches beyond measure. I have health, happiness, love and the satisfaction of knowing I have chased my dreams and tried to help others along the way.

When I started this journey I recalled how the lyrics of a song from the old Broadway musical, Seesaw, suddenly popped into my head at one of the worst moments in my life. I reckon they were pretty prophetic. It really doesn't matter where you start but where you finish. And, in keeping with the words of that song, I believe I really have finished on top.

THE END

Luath Press Limited

committed to publishing well written books worth reading

LUATH PRESS takes its name from Robert Burns, whose little collie Luath (*Gael.*, swift or nimble) tripped up Jean Armour at a wedding and gave him the chance to speak to the woman who was to be his wife and the abiding love of his life. Burns called one of the 'Twa Dogs' Luath after Cuchullin's hunting dog in Ossian's *Fingal*. Luath Press was established in 1981 in the heart of Burns country, and is now based a few steps up the road from Burns' first lodgings on Edinburgh's Royal Mile. Luath offers you distinctive writing with a hint of unexpected pleasures.

Most bookshops in the UK, the US, Canada, Australia, New Zealand and parts of Europe, either carry our books in stock or can order them for you. To order direct from us, please send a £sterling cheque, postal order, international money order or your credit card details (number, address of cardholder and expiry date) to us at the address below. Please add post and packing as follows: UK – £1.00 per delivery address; overseas surface mail – £2.50 per delivery address; overseas airmail – £3.50 for the first book to each delivery address, plus £1.00 for each additional book by airmail to the same address. If your order is a gift, we will happily enclose your card or message at no extra charge.

Luath Press Limited
543/2 Castlehill
The Royal Mile
Edinburgh EH1 2ND
Scotland
Telephone: 0131 225 4326 (24 hours)
Fax: 0131 225 4324
email: sales@luath.co.uk
Website: www.luath.co.uk

The Crisis of Capitalism in Inter-War Glasgow:

Five Realist Novels

To Dear Shona

With love from

Eril Smorgana